Albert
EINSTEIN
and Relativity
for Kids

Albert EINSTEIN
and Relativity
for Kids

His Life and Ideas with 21 Activities
and Thought Experiments

Jerome Pohlen

CHICAGO
REVIEW
PRESS

Published by Chicago Review Press, Incorporated

814 North Franklin Street

Chicago, Illinois 60610

ISBN 978-1-61374-028-6

Library of Congress Cataloging-in-Publication Data

Pohlen, Jerome, author.

Albert Einstein and relativity for kids : his life and ideas with 21 activities and thought experiments /
   Jerome Pohlen. — First edition.

pages cm

Audience: 9 & up

Audience: Grade 4 to 6

Includes bibliographical references and index.

ISBN 978-1-61374-028-6 (pbk.)

1. Einstein, Albert, 1879-1955—Juvenile literature. 2. Physicists—Biography—Juvenile literature.
   3. Relativity (Physics)—Experiments—Juvenile literature. I. Title.

QC16.E5P64 2012

530.092—dc23

[B]

2012021342

Cover and interior design: Monica Baziuk

Front cover photographs: Albert Einstein, © Bettmann/Corbis; clock tower, Jerome Pohlen; Space-time
warp, iStockphoto © Arpad Benedek; Einstein tower, Potsdam, iStockphoto © Andreas Bauer; M31 galaxy,
NASA Chandra Space Telescope Collection; pocketwatch, Shutterstock © Tatiana Popova.

Personality rights of ALBERT EINSTEIN are used with permission of The Hebrew University of Jerusalem.
Represented exclusively by GreenLight.

Back cover photographs: Solar eclipse, Courtesy NASA Astronomy Picture of the Day Collection; train,
Shutterstock © makspogonii; Einstein family, Courtesy of the Leo Baeck Institute, New York (F 5373M).

Interior illustrations: Mark Baziuk

Printed in the United States of America

5   4   3   2

For my father, Joseph Pohlen,
who showed me how much fun science can be

Contents

Time Line

1876	August 8, parents Hermann Einstein and Pauline Koch marry
1879	March 14, Albert Einstein born in Ulm, Germany
1881	November 18, sister Maria (Maja) Einstein born
1887	Michelson-Morley experiment fails to show the presence of an "ether"
1894	The Einsteins move to Italy
1895–1896	Albert attends high school in Aarau
1896–1900	Einstein attends the Zurich Polytechnic Institute
1902	January, Lieserl Einstein born in Novi Sad, Austria-Hungary
	June 23, Einstein begins work at the Swiss Patent Office
	October 10, Hermann Einstein dies in Milan
1903	January 6, Einstein and Mileva Marić marry in Bern
1904	May 14, Hans Albert Einstein born in Bern
1905	Special Theory of Relativity published during Einstein's "Miracle Year"
1909	Einstein becomes an associate professor at the University of Zurich
1910	July 28, Eduard Einstein born in Zurich
1911	The Einsteins move to Prague, where Einstein teaches at German University
	The first Solvay Conference held in Brussels, Belgium
1912	The Einsteins return to Zurich when Einstein accepts position at the Zurich Polytechnic Institute
1914	The Einsteins move to Berlin, Germany
	The Einsteins separate and Mileva returns to Switzerland with Hans Albert and Eduard
	World War I breaks out

1915	Einstein announces the General Theory of Relativity to the Royal Prussian Academy of Sciences
1916	General Theory of Relativity published in the *Annalen der Physik*
1918	November 11, World War I ends with the signing of the Armistice
1919	February 14, Albert and Mileva divorce
	May 29, eclipse confirms General Theory of Relativity
	June 2, Albert and Elsa Löwenthal marry in Berlin; Einstein adopts Elsa's daughters, Ilse and Margot
	November 6, Astronomer Royal Frank Dyson announces Eddington's findings
1920	February 20, Pauline Einstein dies
1922	Einstein receives the Nobel Prize for physics . . . of 1921
1933	Hitler comes to power in Germany while Einstein is in the United States
1936	December 20, Elsa Einstein dies in Princeton
1939	August 2, Einstein sends a letter to President Roosevelt encouraging the development of the atomic bomb; writes another letter March 7, 1940
	September 1, World War II breaks out when Germany invades Poland
1940	October 1, Einstein becomes a US citizen
1941	December 7, Japan bombs Pearl Harbor; the United States enters World War II the next day
1945	May 7, Germany surrenders to the Allies
	August 6 and 9, the United States drops atomic bombs on Hiroshima and Nagasaki, Japan
	August 15, Japan surrenders and World War II ends
1946	Einstein named president of the Emergency Committee of Atomic Scientists
1948	August 4, Mileva Marić Einstein dies in Zurich
1951	June 25, paralyzed since 1948 by a stroke, Maja Einstein dies in Princeton
1952	Einstein declines to become the second president of Israel
1955	April 18, Albert Einstein dies in Princeton, New Jersey
1965	October 25, Eduard Einstein dies in Zurich
1973	July 26, Hans Albert Einstein dies in Massachusetts

Acknowledgments

THIS PROJECT began years ago with all those forever underpaid Douglas County teachers who fostered my love of science and math, including Steven Williams, Dick Wright, Jodene Bartolo, Doug Kissler, Ann McNulty, Kathleen Gilbert, Marty Bowen, Malcolm Hovde, John Moos, and Debbie Wadsworth, as well as everyone associated with the Frontiers of Science Institute at the University of Northern Colorado: Bill Koch, Mary Beth Endres, Paul Wharry, Mary Lou Whisenand, Phil Gleckler, and Paul Lightsey.

My thanks to the reviewers who helped me fine-tune the manuscript—Juan Gonzalez, Lisa Reardon, and Tom Vose. To everyone at Chicago Review Press who worked to make this book a reality—Michelle Schoob, Monica Baziuk, Gerilee Hundt, Allison Felus, Jon Hahn, and Caitlin Eck—thank you for all your hard work. But in particular, I am indebted to my longtime editor, Cynthia Sherry, for supporting my writing for more than a decade. An author couldn't ask for a better champion.

And finally, thank you Jim Frost and my parents, Joseph and Barbara Pohlen.

Note to Readers

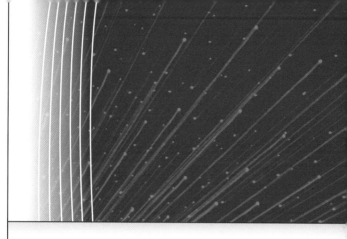

Thought Experiments

IMAGINE THAT you were to walk into a brick wall. Would it hurt? Of course! Would you need to walk into a brick wall to convince yourself of this? No, you could figure it out without actually having to do it. You know that brick walls are hard. You know that if something hits you in the nose it hurts. So, if your nose were to hit a very hard brick wall, it would hurt.

Congratulations—you've just performed a *thought experiment*. Albert Einstein was famous for using thought experiments to develop his theories and to explain his ideas to other people. He would imagine trains traveling at nearly the speed of light (this was long before rockets) and elevators falling down bottomless shafts or traveling through space. What would people on those trains and in those elevators experience?

In this book you will be asked to perform several thought experiments to better understand Einstein's theories. They will be marked with a  .

Read the description of each imaginary experiment, then try to answer the questions that follow before reading further. Most of the thought experiments in this book are Einstein's own, so they will be your chance to match wits with a genius.

"*Imagination is more important than knowledge. Knowledge is limited. Imagination encircles the world.*"

—Einstein

Albert Einstein at a
patent office desk, 1905.

Introduction

The Patent Clerk

TUCKED AWAY on the third floor of the Postal and Telegraph Building near the train station in Bern, Switzerland, Albert Einstein scribbled away. "Whenever anyone would come by, I would cram my notes into my desk drawer and pretend to work on my office work," he later admitted. "I was able to do a full day's work in only two or three hours. The remaining part of the day I would work on my own ideas."

What sort of ideas? Everything from the size of atoms to the structure of the universe. Just a few years earlier he had graduated from college where he had studied physics, but nobody would hire him. Einstein had worked as a substitute teacher and a tutor, but those jobs barely paid his bills. He got this position at the Swiss Patent Office only because his friend's father had put in a good word for him.

So Einstein scribbled away when nobody was looking, and when he got home he wrote even more. He bounced his ideas off his wife, who was a talented mathematician, and a few of his friends and coworkers, but ultimately he was an *Einspänner*—a one-horse cart. A loner.

But this one-horse cart, with little more than the force of his gifted mind, would pull physics into the modern era and beyond.

Albert Einstein (front row, third from right) and his elementary school classmates. He is one of only two children smiling. Courtesy of the Leo Baeck Institute, New York (F 5308E)

A Curious and Independent Child

1879–1901

"*I have no special talents.*
I am only passionately curious."

—Einstein

"**Much too fat!**" said Grandma Jette, seeing her grandson Albert for the first time. "Much too fat!" she repeated. But Pauline Einstein wasn't worried about her baby's body. She did, however, think his head looked odd. It was too large, and had a funny shape—it stuck out at the back. Was that normal?

This was her first child, and it was natural that she would feel concerned. But her doctor told her Albert was perfectly fine. Little did she know what brilliant ideas would one day come out of her son's strange-looking head.

Hermann and Pauline

ALBERT EINSTEIN was born on Friday, March 14, 1879. His parents, Hermann and Pauline Einstein, lived in a small apartment at 20 Bahnhofstrasse (Railway Station Street) in Ulm, Germany. Like most children at the time, Albert was born at home.

The Einsteins had been married for two and a half years before Albert arrived. Pauline Koch was the daughter of a wealthy grain merchant and was the youngest of four children. She was just 18 years old when she wed Hermann Einstein, who was 11 years older. They were married on August 8, 1876, in the town of Cannstatt, where Pauline had grown up. After the wedding they made their first home in the village of Buchau.

Though Jews had lived in Germany for about 1,500 years, it wasn't until the 1860s that they were allowed to become full German citizens. Before then, Jews could not hold certain jobs or own property in Germany. Many lived in rural villages as the Einsteins did. But as Germany changed, Jews migrated to the cities for new opportunities. A year after they were married, Hermann and Pauline moved to Ulm, an old medieval city with winding streets on the banks of the Danube River. Here Hermann sold featherbeds for a company he owned with his cousins.

The Einsteins were considered nonobservant Jews. They did not keep a kosher house-

Einstein's Ulm birthplace. It was destroyed during Allied bombings in World War II. Hebrew University of Jerusalem, Albert Einstein Archives, courtesy AIP Emilio Segre Visual Archives

hold, nor did they regularly attend synagogue. Hermann and Pauline dismissed many Jewish traditions, but they shared the value the Jewish people placed on knowledge and education. Albert would also hold these values for most of his life.

Everyone agreed that Hermann and Pauline had a happy, middle-class marriage. People who knew them described Pauline as affectionate yet stubborn. Hermann was hopelessly optimistic, despite the financial ups and downs of his businesses.

LEFT: Hermann Einstein. RIGHT: Pauline Einstein.
Hebrew University of Jerusalem, Albert Einstein Archives, courtesy AIP Emilio Segre Visual Archives

Munich and Maja

A YEAR after Albert was born, Hermann was invited by his brother Jakob to open an electrical supply company in Munich. What luck! The featherbed business was failing, and electricity was the industry of the future. The light-bulb had just been invented, and everyone wanted the new technology. Besides, Hermann had always loved math and science.

When the Einsteins first moved to Munich they rented a third-floor apartment in the city. It was here that Albert's sister Maria was born on November 18, 1881. When Albert saw her for the first time he asked, "But where are its wheels?" He had been told that his new sister would be someone he could play with, so he assumed she was a toy. She turned out to be something even better—Maja, as Maria became known, became Albert's closest friend.

The Einsteins probably hoped that a little sister would draw Albert out of his shell. Though he was two and a half years old, he barely spoke. The family's maid even called him *der Depperte*—"the dopey one"—when nobody was around. Years later, Einstein explained, "When I was between two and three, I formed the ambition to speak in full sentences." To do this, he would practice what he wanted to say. "Every sentence he uttered, no matter how routine, he repeated to himself softly, moving his lips," Maja recalled. Even when he did speak, he talked softly and slowly. He continued this habit until he was seven years old.

Pauline Einstein encouraged her two young children to be independent. After showing Albert around the neighborhood, she allowed him to walk alone on the streets of Munich . . . starting when he was four years old. But, just to be safe, she had one of her friends secretly follow her son until she was confident he could make it on his own.

Albert's mother also wanted her son to learn to play an instrument, so he was given a violin at age six. Pauline Einstein was an accomplished pianist, but her love of music did not immediately rub off on her child. His first violin tutor fled the house after Albert threw a tantrum, and a chair, during a lesson. It wasn't until he heard one of Mozart's sonatas at age 13 that he began to share his mother's passion. Years later he said, "If I were not a physicist, I would probably be a musician. I often think in music. I live my daydreams in music. I see my life in terms of music."

Life at the Einstein home must have been stimulating for young Albert. His father and Uncle Jakob would bring home inventions, tools, and instruments from their factory. Once when Albert was sick in bed at the age of five, his father gave him a compass to play with. Albert shook the compass and turned it around, but its needle always pointed north. "I can still remem-

Albert, age five, and Maja, age three.
© Bettmann/Corbis

ber . . . that this experience made a deep and lasting impression on me. Something deeply hidden had to be behind things," he recalled.

Off to School

ALBERT EINSTEIN was tutored at home until he was six years old. By the time he was ready for school, his family had moved to a new home in Sendling, a suburb of Munich. Uncle Jakob's family bought the house next door and the two families shared a back garden where Albert enjoyed playing with chickens and pigeons. The Einstein brothers' company, J. Einstein & Cie, opened a nearby factory in 1885 and had 200 employees. They had just been awarded the first contract to light Munich's Bavarian Oktoberfest. Business was good.

On October 1, 1885, Albert started classes at Petersschule—Peter's School—a nearby Catholic elementary school. He started in second grade and was a good student. The only subject he didn't much like was gym.

Though classrooms at Petersschule had as many as 70 students, Albert didn't make friends unless he had to. As one of the only Jewish children in the school, he faced teasing from classmates, and worse. "Physical attacks and insults on the way home from school were frequent," Einstein remembered.

Compass and Magnet

USE A compass to re-create one of Albert Einstein's earliest experiments.

You'll Need
➤ Compass
➤ Bar magnet (optional)

Use a compass in your home to determine which direction north is. Hold the compass level with the floor and wait for the needle to stop moving.

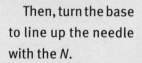

Then, turn the base to line up the needle with the *N*.

Next, move outside or to another floor and try again. Is north still in the same direction?

Your compass is aligning with the weak north–south magnetic field of the Earth. But if you move it close to a stronger magnetic field created by a magnet, it will point in a new direction. Magnets are used in many objects around your home, though you may not be able to see them because they're *inside* what you're looking at—think "motors." Use your compass to find a stronger magnetic field in your home.

Finally, if you have a bar magnet, use it to experiment with the compass needle. Holding the magnet an inch from the compass, to which end, north or south, does the compass needle point? (Warning: Do not touch your magnet to the compass—it could permanently throw off the needle.) How far away does the magnet have to be before the compass realigns with Earth's magnetic field?

House of Cards

A S A CHILD, Albert enjoyed building complex card houses, some as tall as 14 stories. How high do you think you could go?

You'll Need
➤ 2 decks of cards (or more)

The most common method to build a card house uses two A-frame pairs topped by another card. This works best on a rough surface, such as a rug, rather than a smooth one, such as a glass tabletop. It also helps to use older cards that are not as slippery as new ones.

Continue building out, and up.

Can you construct a house that uses all 52 cards in a deck? How about two decks? Or can you come up with a better method to build a card house?

Albert wasn't like other students who enjoyed sports and playing soldier. In fact, from a very early age he rejected anything military. One afternoon his class was taken out of the building to line up along a parade route to wave flags as the German Royal Guards passed by. "When I grow up, I don't want to be one of those poor people," he later told his parents.

It wasn't just militarism that Albert didn't care for; he wasn't fond of any authority figure. His dislike of strict discipline only grew stronger when he was enrolled in the Luitpold-Gymnasium in 1888. (In Germany a gymnasium is a secondary school.) "The teachers at the elementary school seemed to me like drill sergeants, and the teachers at the gymnasium like lieutenants," he remembered.

Albert's new classmates weren't much nicer. Students called him *Biedermeier*, which translates as "Honest John." Or, in another word, nerd. If it bothered him, he didn't show it.

Einstein didn't find most of the classes at the gymnasium very challenging. He liked math, physics, and Latin but wasn't interested in history, geography, French, or Greek. He preferred instead to have intellectual discussions at home with Uncle Jakob (who introduced him to algebra) and a family friend, Max Talmud.

There is a tradition in Jewish culture that a family should invite a religious scholar for dinner on the Friday night Sabbath. The Einsteins made their own tradition by inviting Talmud, a medical student at Munich University, for their Thursday night meal. Talmud became 10-year-old Albert's unofficial tutor. Each week he would bring books on science, math, and philosophy for Albert to read, and they would discuss them the following week. Albert's favorite was a series of 21 books by Aaron Bernstein: *The People's Books on Natural Science*. Among other topics, Bernstein wrote about the speed of light, and what it might be like to ride alongside a signal in a telegraph wire. In one book he asked readers to do a thought experiment on the motion of a bullet shot into a moving train—how would the bullet's path look different to somebody on the train compared to the person who fired it?

When Albert was 12, Talmud gave him a geometry book, Euclid's *Elements*, which he devoured with "breathless suspense." Albert would work on problems all week and show them to Talmud each Thursday night. Albert then moved on to calculus. "Soon the flight of his mathematical genius was so high that I could no longer follow," Talmud admitted.

Italy

Almost as quickly as the Einstein brothers' electrical business had grown, it began to fail.

Isaac Newton (1643–1727) and Newtonian Physics

When Einstein was a child, Newtonian physics ruled the day. Isaac Newton was a brilliant British mathematician and physicist who came up with three laws of motion, laws that could explain everything from an apple falling from a tree to the revolution of planets around the sun. They are:

1. A body will remain at rest or in uniform motion (in a straight line at a constant speed) unless acted upon by a force.

Isaac Newton. Library of Congress Prints and Photographs Division (LC-USZ62-10191)

2. A body will accelerate in proportion to the force acting upon it, and in the same direction. As a mathematical formula, this is written

Force = mass × acceleration

3. For every action there is an equal and opposite reaction.

Newton came up with his three laws in 1666 while spending a year in the English countryside. He had fled Cambridge University, near London, when the school closed its doors after students started dying from the plague. As scary as that sounds, it did give him time to focus. And Newton didn't just come up with new ideas about motion. He also wrote his theory of gravitation, invented a new form of math called calculus, and explored the behavior of light, called optics.

People later called this Newton's *Annus mirabilis*—"Miracle Year" in Latin. He was only 24 years old at the time. (Einstein would have his own *Annus mirabilis* in 1905.)

Even though Einstein's General Theory of Relativity replaced Newtonian physics for astronomers looking at stars and scientists studying the atom, for the rest of us, Newton's formulas still work just fine, even if they are *slightly* off. Even Einstein admitted this later in life. "Newton forgive me," he wrote. "You found the only way which, in your age, was just about possible for a man of highest thought and creative power."

Munich to Milan

When Einstein was a teenager, the easiest and fastest way to get from one city to another was by train. And while it may not be as fast as by airplane today, traveling by train in Europe is still very easy. Can you plan a trip from Munich to Milan?

You'll Need
➤ Internet access
➤ Adult permission

Imagine that you live in Munich, Germany, and that you want to buy a ticket to travel to Milan, Italy. You hope to leave tomorrow.

With an adult's permission, go online to the Eurail website, www.eurail.com. Click on the "Planning" link on the Eurail page. Once there, you will be able to input the date, departure city, and destination for your trip. For your departure city choose Munich (München), and for your destination select Milan (Central).

After you submit your request, you will receive many different travel options. The times are shown in "military time," meaning that afternoon times don't restart counting at noon, but continue straight through the 24 hours of the day: 9:30 AM = 09:30, but 9:30 PM = 21:30 (12:00 + 9:30).

Look at each option, being sure to view the "Trip Details" to tell you how many times you'll have to change trains, and where. Then see if you can answer the following questions:

1. Which trip is fastest?

2. Does the first train to leave Munich arrive first in Milan? If not, can you figure out why?

3. Where do you have to transfer from one train to another?

4. Germany and Italy do not share a border. Does your trip travel through Austria or Switzerland?

Other companies were getting into the industry and competition became fierce. In 1894 they lost a bid to install electric lighting in the central district of Munich and the company went bankrupt.

The Einsteins then made a tough decision. At the time Italy was not as "electrified" as Germany, so Jakob and Hermann decided to move both families to Milan and start over. Albert, who was then 15, was left behind with distant relatives to finish his studies at the gymnasium.

Before long, Albert was miserable. He missed Maja and the rest of his family. And school was even worse. His homeroom teacher, Joseph Degenhart, told him in front of the class that he wouldn't amount to anything. Degenhart didn't like Albert's attitude. "You sit there in the back row smiling. And that undermines the respect a teacher needs from his class," he said.

So Albert came up with a plan. First, he got Max Talmud's older brother Bernard, who was a doctor, to write him a note saying he suffered from "neurasthenic exhaustion" and needed a break from school. *Immediately*. He also got his math teacher to write him a letter of recommendation, saying he had mastered the gymnasium's math curriculum. And then on December 29, 1894, Albert boarded a train headed for Italy. When he arrived unannounced at his parents' home in Milan, a confident and independent young man, Pauline

Einstein might have had second thoughts about teaching her son to walk alone on the streets of Munich.

Albert told his parents he did not want to return to Munich. What's more, he wanted to renounce his German citizenship. Every German male who was not in school at the age of 16 was required to enlist in the army, and he was 15. (Those who were still in school had to enlist after graduation.) His parents listened, but at first they did not support his wish.

Without classes to attend, Albert spent some days helping out in his father's factory, but more often he would wander the Italian countryside or hang out in libraries and museums. It wasn't long before Hermann demanded that his son start thinking about a profession. Albert decided he wanted to attend the Zurich Polytechnic Institute (known today as the Eidgenössische Technische Hochschule, or ETH). Most people just called it the Poly. Luckily, the Poly did not require its students to have a high school diploma, only that they pass the entrance exams. And be at least 18 years old.

But with the help of a family friend and the letter from Albert's math teacher, the Poly decided to overlook Albert's young age. He took the exams in the fall of 1885, and though he passed the physics and mathematics portions, he failed on the French, botany, zoology, literature, and chemistry portions. Neverthe-less, he was offered admittance . . . if he received his secondary school diploma.

There was no way Albert would agree to return to the gymnasium in Germany. Where would he go?

Aarau

Albert's failure to get into the Poly turned out to be a stroke of good luck. That fall he enrolled in the Swiss Cantonal School of Aargau in the town of Aarau, west of Zurich. Unlike at the gymnasium, at Aarau he was encouraged to think independently. Years later he said,

That institution left an unforgettable impression on me; the comparison with the six years I spent in a German high school run with an iron fist made me truly understand just how superior is an education based on freedom of choice and self-accountability over an education that relies on regimentation, external authority, and ambition.

It was here that Einstein first asked himself what it would be like to travel on a beam of light. Would the light wave stand still? And if it did, what would *that* look like? If he held a mirror out in front of himself at that speed, would he see his reflection? The teachers in

Aarau even had a word for what he was doing: *Gedankenexperiment*—a thought experiment.

Because his family was still in Italy, Albert stayed with the family of his Greek and history professor, Jost Winteler; his wife, Pauline; and their seven children. The Wintelers welcomed him into their home, and Albert even began calling them Papa and Mamerl (Little Mother). On weekends they all took long hikes in the mountains where they would fly kites and learn to identify local plants and animals.

When Albert went home during the school's Christmas break in 1895, he again asked his father to help him renounce his German citizenship, and this time Hermann agreed. Albert Einstein's German citizenship was officially revoked on January 28, 1896. But he was still too young to apply for Swiss citizenship. Albert would have to wait until 1899 to start that process. For the time being, he was a boy without a country.

Albert graduated from high school second in his class in June 1896. In his final essay for French class he wrote:

> *If I am lucky and pass my exams, I will enroll in the Zurich Polytechnic. I will stay there for four years to study mathematics and physics. I suppose I will become a teacher in these fields of science, opting for the theoretical part of these sciences. . . . I am attracted by the independence offered by the profession of science.*

He retook the entrance exams for the Poly, and this time he passed.

Einstein attended this high school in Aarau.

College Life

Back when Einstein attended the Zurich Polytechnic Institute, it was very different from most colleges of today. In four years of study, students were required to take only two rounds of tests—their intermediate exams halfway through, and their finals. Students were expected, but not required, to attend lectures and labs. There was no homework. There were no pop quizzes or papers to write, except for a final thesis. For a daydreamer, it was perfect—and dangerous.

Albert Einstein moved into a rooming house at 4 Unionstrasse—Union Street—in the fall and started classes on October 29, 1896. He was 17, six months younger than he would have needed to be had the Poly not bent the rules for him. Wealthy Aunt Julie from his mother's side of the family sent him an allowance of 100 Swiss francs a month for expenses. (He saved some of that money each month for the application fee to become a Swiss citizen.)

Though there were about a thousand students attending the Poly with Einstein, he was one of only five in his class who were studying physics. Most of the school's students studied to be engineers or teachers. Technically, Einstein was studying to be a physics teacher, not a physicist, even though he did not take classes on education.

Unlike his days at the gymnasium, at the Poly Einstein made many friends. During one Saturday music recital he met Marcel Grossmann, a mathematics student, who became a lifelong friend. And had he not met Grossmann, Einstein may never have finished college.

Grossmann was a serious student who attended every lecture and took detailed notes. Einstein, on the other hand, preferred his own course of study. He spent a lot of time reading up on subjects he found more interesting

The Zurich Polytechnic Institute—the Poly.

than those being taught in the classroom. As his intermediate exams approached, Einstein realized he would have to catch up to his classmates, so he borrowed Grossmann's notes to cram for the tests.

The plan worked. Einstein scored first in his class on his intermediate examinations. Still, he was smart enough to know that Grossmann had saved his hide. "I would rather not speculate on what would have become of me without these notes," he later admitted.

Grossmann, who placed second, credited Einstein's intellect. Not long after meeting Einstein he told his father, "Einstein will be a great man someday."

Mileva Marić

OF THE four other people studying physics with Einstein, one was Mileva Marić. She was only the fifth woman ever to enroll at the Poly to study physics.

Marić came from Novi Sad in Austria-Hungary, part of today's Serbia. Her father, Milos, was a former army soldier who later become a court clerk, and then a judge; her mother, Marija, came from a wealthy Serbian family.

Mileva was born on December 19, 1875, the first of three children. She was born with a dislocated left hip, which caused one leg to be shorter than the other, so when she walked she limped.

Milos and Marija Marić always wanted the best for their children. Mileva showed a gift for math and science throughout school, but high school was as far as she could go. In the late 1800s, women were not allowed to attend college in Austria-Hungary. In fact, Switzerland was the only German-speaking country where Marić could even apply.

Marić originally enrolled at the University of Zurich as a medical student, but a semester later she transferred to the Poly, starting at the same time as Einstein. While there she lived in the Engelbrecht pension (boardinghouse) at 50 Plattenstrasse. She was a serious and dedicated student.

During their first year at the Poly they were strictly classmates, though Einstein did enjoy dropping by the Engelbrecht pension to play his violin while Marić accompanied him on the piano or sang. Everyone said she had a beautiful voice.

Perhaps worried about her growing feelings for Einstein, or his feelings for her, Marić transferred to the University of Heidelberg the following fall. Less than a year later, she returned. Soon they had given each other nicknames—he would call her Doxerl (Dollie) and she called him Johonzel (Johnnie). They were an item.

Mileva Marić, 1896.

Burning Bridges

EINSTEIN'S NEW romance didn't improve his attitude toward his classwork. In fact, it made things worse. Einstein (urged on by Marić) soon convinced himself that he was above the dusty, outdated lectures of his Poly instructors. Einstein's math professor, Hermann Minkowski, would later call him a "lazy dog."

Jean Pernet, the instructor for his Physical Experiments for Beginners lab, was less kind. In July 1899 Einstein caused an explosion during class. The blast injured his right hand and required stitches, and he couldn't play the violin for a while. "You're enthusiastic but hopeless at physics," Pernet told him. "For your own good you should switch to something else, medicine, maybe, literature, or law." Einstein didn't follow this career advice, though he did promise himself to focus on *theoretical* physics.

Worst of all, Einstein butted heads with his physics professor, Heinrich Weber, the same man who had helped him get into the Poly before he was old enough. Einstein thought Weber was behind the times because he did not teach about the work of James Clerk Maxwell, a physicist who had done groundbreaking work on electromagnetic radiation, first discovered by Michael Faraday.

"You're a very clever boy, Einstein, an extremely clever boy," Weber once told him. "But you have one great fault: you'll never let yourself be told anything." And he did mean

Michael Faraday (1791–1867)

Michael Faraday, the son of a Scottish blacksmith, had no formal science education, yet he became the first scientist to discover the relationship between electricity and magnetism. In 1821 he found that if he passed an electric current through a stationary (still) wire near a magnet, the magnet would turn. In the same way, if he held the magnet still and passed a current through the wire, the wire would move. These phenomena would later be used to create the first electric motors.

For physicists, Faraday's discovery was even more profound, for he had unified two previously unconnected fields of science. During his career, Faraday created the first transformer and the first dynamo. He also revolutionized chemistry through the study of electrolysis. He was the first person to sprinkle iron filings over a magnet to show its magnetic field, and he also discovered that the shock given off by an eel was static electricity.

James Clerk Maxwell (1831–1879)

Though Michael Faraday discovered the relationship between electricity and magnetism, it was James Clerk Maxwell (also a Scotsman) who translated Faraday's work into mathematical terms that physicists could use.

Maxwell also determined that an electrical current travels at the same speed as visible light. He produced the world's first permanent color photograph in 1861, figured out why Saturn's rings were stable, and developed the kinetic theory of gases.

Where Faraday took an experimental approach, Maxwell used thought experiments and complex math to develop most of his theories. Not surprisingly, as a teenager Einstein was fascinated by Maxwell's work. As an adult, he would prove Maxwell's theories about light being a wave traveling through an "ether" wrong.

anything. When Einstein turned in his senior research thesis, it was written on the wrong paper. Weber demanded that he rewrite it.

All those afternoons hanging out in local cafés, hiking through the nearby mountains, and sailing on Lake Zurich came back to haunt Einstein, and not even Grossmann's notes could help him. In July 1900, after taking his final examinations, Einstein graduated from the Zurich Polytechnic, fourth in a class of five. Marić placed fifth, and she did not test well enough to graduate.

Alone and Unemployed

AFTER GRADUATION, Albert Einstein found himself abruptly tossed into the "real world." His aunt in Genoa stopped sending him an allowance. Back in Italy his father's most recent business enterprise had failed; his family was in no position to support him while he looked for work.

Einstein wanted to find a job at a university, perhaps as an assistant in a physics department. He sent out job inquiries to professors all over Europe, but with no luck. Not even the Poly wanted him. *Especially* the Poly. "From what people tell me, I am not in the good graces of any of my former teachers," Einstein wrote in a letter to a friend.

Meanwhile, Albert and Mileva's relationship grew more serious, and they began to talk of marriage. When they were apart, they sent each other love letters. "I am so lucky to have found you—a creature who is my equal, and who is as strong and independent as I am," Einstein wrote. And on some occasions he penned corny poetry for her:

Oh My! That Johnnie boy!
So crazy with desire.
While thinking of his Dollie,
His pillow catches fire.

Pauline Einstein didn't share her son's affection for Mileva. She didn't think Mileva was good enough for Albert, and told him so. Mileva wasn't Jewish; she was Eastern Orthodox. She was "old," three whole years older than Albert, and Pauline thought she was unattractive. Once, while visiting his family, Einstein referred to Mileva as his wife, even though they had not married. Albert wrote to Mileva about what happened next:

Mama threw herself on the bed, buried her head in the pillow, and wept like a child. After regaining her composure, she immediately shifted to a desperate attack: "You're ruining your future and destroying your opportunities." "No decent family would want her." "If she becomes pregnant, you'll be in a real mess."

College students in 1899 (left to right): Marcel Grossmann, Albert Einstein, Gustav Geissler, and Eugen Grossmann. Hebrew University of Jerusalem, Albert Einstein Archives, courtesy AIP Emilio Segre Visual Archives

Pauline Einstein's fear soon became a reality. In the spring of 1901, Mileva Marić got pregnant. Albert and Mileva decided that Mileva would return to her parents' home in Novi Sad to have the baby. Before leaving Zurich, Mileva took her final exams a second time, and failed them again.

In January 1902 Mileva gave birth to a girl, Lieserl—Little Lisa. Very little is known about what happened to Lieserl because Einstein and Marić kept her birth secret from all but their closest friends and family. Marić returned to Switzerland without her. Was Lieserl given up for adoption? Did Marić's parents, relatives, or best friend, Helene Savić, raise her, perhaps until Albert and Mileva married?

Based on a letter Einstein wrote in September 1903, historians believe Lieserl contracted scarlet fever. This serious disease often led to death, and even those who survived could be left with disabilities such as deafness or brain damage. Whether Lieserl survived or not, there is no record of her ever growing up. (Einstein's letter wasn't revealed until 1986.)

A month after Lieserl was born in Austria-Hungary, Einstein's application to become a Swiss citizen was approved. He needed this if he was to find a job in Switzerland, and he desperately needed a job. "I decided the following about our future," Einstein wrote Marić. "I will look for a position immediately, no matter how modest it is. My scientific goals and my personal vanity will not prevent me from accepting even the most subordinate position."

And he did. Einstein took a three-month job as a substitute math teacher at a technical school in Winterthur. After that he tutored a student from England at a boarding school in Schaffhausen. It didn't pay much, and it lasted only a few months—Einstein got into an argument with his boss and was fired.

"[Bern is] an ancient, exquisitely cozy city, in which one can live exactly as in Zurich." —Einstein

The Patent Office and the Miracle Year

1901–1909

"**Dear Marcel**," **Einstein** wrote. "When I found your letter yesterday I was deeply moved by your devotion and compassion which do not let you forget an old, unlucky friend." Albert's former classmate who had taken such detailed notes had learned that there would be a job opening soon at the Swiss Patent Office in Bern. Marcel Grossmann's father was a friend of Friedrich Haller, who ran the office.

The elder Grossmann suggested Haller speak to Einstein, and Albert took the train to Bern for the two-hour interview. Though his training was in physics, Einstein had picked up enough technical knowledge from his experience at his father and uncle's factory that he convinced Haller

Capillary Action

HAVE YOU ever observed capillary action . . . in action? In this activity, you will test three different tubes as they "pull" water up, against gravity.

You'll Need
➤ 3 short, clear tubes with different diameters
➤ Clear tape
➤ Glass of water
➤ Food coloring

First, find three clear tubes with different diameters—drinking straws, plastic ballpoint pens, aquarium tubes. They should all be about the same length and be open at both ends.

Align the bottom of the tubes, smallest diameter to largest diameter, and tape them together.

Add food coloring to a glass of water. This will make the water easier to see when it is in the tubes.

Slowly lower the bottom of the three taped tubes into water. Hold the tubes still and observe how high the water rises up into them.

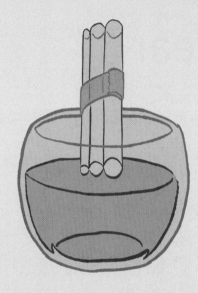

What can you say about the diameter of a tube and how well it can pull up water through capillary action?

Answer: *The smaller a tube's diameter, the higher up it will pull a column of water.*

to give him a chance. Yet nothing moved that smoothly or quickly through the Swiss governmental bureaucracy. Einstein would have to wait for an official appointment.

The Olympia Academy

THOUGH HE was out of school and not working at a university, Albert Einstein never stopped thinking about physics.

In December 1900 he had submitted his first paper to the prestigious *Annalen der Physik*—the *Journal of Physics*—and it was published in March 1901. It had to do with capillary action, the force that "pulls" a liquid up a tube. Einstein believed that liquids with different atomic weights would experience capillary action differently. It turns out he was wrong, though nobody at the time, including Einstein, could prove it.

Far more important than what Einstein wrote in his paper was the fact that it was published in the *Annalen der Physik*. The journal was read by physicists everywhere, and it might help him get a job at a university. Someday.

In the meantime, Einstein waited. The position at the Swiss Patent Office seemed promising, so he moved to Bern in late 1901 to wait for the appointment to come through. He lived in a first-floor apartment at 32 Gerechtigkeitsgasse (Justice Lane). Einstein's old family friend, Max Talmud, visited him and later admitted, "His environment betrayed a good deal of poverty. He lived in a small, poorly furnished room."

To pay the bills, Einstein put an ad in a local paper on February 5, 1902: "Private lessons in Mathematics and Physics for students and pupils given most thoroughly by Albert Einstein, holder of the Fed. Polyt. teacher's diploma. . . . Trial lessons free." Two men responded to the ad, an architect and an engineer. Neither pupil made Einstein much money.

A few months later Einstein reran the ad and Maurice Solovine responded. A Romanian philosophy student at the University of Bern, Solovine wanted to learn a little physics. Upon meeting the men talked for over two hours and became fast friends. They decided to get together the following night, just to discuss topics of their choosing.

Soon they were joined by Conrad Habicht, a friend of Einstein's from his time teaching at Schaffhausen. (Habicht was working on a PhD in math at the university.) The three gave their weekly gatherings a name: the Akademie Olympia—the Olympia Academy. It was as much an excuse for dinner as debate, but they did explore many complex topics. The trio would drink Turkish coffee and eat hard-boiled eggs, sausages, cheese, and fruit, all while arguing late into the night. Sometimes they would hike in the local mountains while discussing philosophy, science, literature, or politics, then set up camp and talk until sunrise. Einstein enjoyed the company.

The Olympia Academy (from left to right): Conrad Habicht, Maurice Solovine, and Albert Einstein. © Underwood & Underwood/Corbis

The Patent Office

ALBERT EINSTEIN'S appointment finally came through on June 16, 1902. Though he had applied for the position of Technical Expert, Second Class, he was hired as a Technical Expert, *Third* Class. It was the lowest position in the office, paying only 3,500 Swiss francs per year. But he had a job. Einstein started a week later, on June 23. He was expected to arrive at work at 8:00 am, six days a week.

Einstein would be given many of the patent office's applications for electrical devices. His boss, Friedrich Haller, told him how to approach his work: "When you pick up an application, think that everything the inventor says is wrong." That was one instruction Einstein didn't need to be told. He questioned *everything*.

When Einstein worked in the patent office, Switzerland was trying to use new electrical technology to synchronize its train system. Many of the patents came across his desk. Bern had already used its central clock tower to synchronize all the city clocks, including those at the train station. But could the same be done for the entire country?

Einstein took the question one step further. Knowing that electricity moved at the speed of light, which was fast but not instantaneous, he knew there could be no way to set all the clocks to the *exact* same time. But he also wondered about the nature of "simultaneity"—when two events happen at the same time. Was it even possible to say two events happened at the same moment? His answer would become central to the Special Theory of Relativity.

The Swiss Patent Office was located on the third floor of this building.

Married Life

IN THE fall of 1902 Einstein received an urgent telegram: his father had suffered a heart attack. He raced to his parents' home in Milan where Hermann lay in bed, near death. Before passing away, Hermann gave his approval for Albert to marry Mileva. Hermann died on October 10, 1902.

Mileva Marić had moved to a town near Bern after giving birth to Lieserl. On January 6, 1903, Albert and Mileva were married in a ceremony at the town's civil registry. Maurice Solovine and Conrad Habicht acted as witnesses. Pauline Einstein did not attend. Neither did Marić's parents.

The Einsteins and the Olympia Academy celebrated into the night, and when the newlyweds returned to the couple's apartment they found that they were locked out. Albert had forgotten his key. They had to wake the landlady to let them in.

In the fall of 1903 the Einsteins rented an apartment in central Bern, near the city's main clock tower. Here the Olympia Academy would sometimes meet, with Mileva as its newest member. She didn't always join in, but when she did she was quite confident, sometimes stamping her feet to make a point. Unfortunately, Habicht graduated and left Bern that December, and Solovine moved away the following spring. The Olympia Academy was no more.

Luckily for Einstein an old friend from Zurich, engineer Michele Besso, was hired by the patent office around the same time. (Einstein had recommended him.) Besso would become the new sounding board for the revolutionary ideas swirling in Einstein's head. Each

The Bern Clock Tower

By a stroke of luck, the route Einstein walked from his new apartment to his job at the patent office passed right by Bern's famous clock tower. Walking toward or away from the tower, he often thought about the nature of time. In his 1905 paper on relativity (page 28), he used the clock tower to explain one of his thought experiments.

The tower was built between 1218 and 1256 as the main gate to the city. The clock was added later, in 1527, just 35 years after Columbus sailed to the New World. It shows not only the time but the date and the position of the zodiac. In 1890 the clock tower was used to electronically synchronize all the clocks in Bern. A decade later, Switzerland did the same for all the clocks in its train system.

The Bern clock tower.

evening the friends would walk home from the office together as Einstein spoke about his theories.

On May 14, 1904, Mileva gave birth to a baby boy, Hans Albert. She later wrote to her friend Helene Savić, "I cannot tell you how much joy [Hans] gives me when he laughs so cheerfully on waking up or when he kicks his legs while taking a bath and makes me afraid he might slip out of my hands."

Albert took his own approach to raising his son. Friends reported that he would rock Hans's cradle with his foot while reading or writing at a nearby table. Whenever he pushed the baby's carriage about the streets of Bern he would carry a small notebook, and if a new idea struck him he would stop pushing and jot down notes.

In September of that year Einstein was finally taken off his probationary period at the patent office and given a 400-franc raise.

The Miracle Year

THOUGH EINSTEIN had been thinking about and studying physics most of his young life, in 1905 the floodgates opened in his mind. Between March and September he wrote five groundbreaking papers that forever changed the way scientists look at the world. Einstein called it the Miracle Year.

Each of Einstein's papers was published in the *Annalen der Physik*. The journal had a policy that it would print future papers from any author it had already published, and Einstein had his capillarity paper under his belt. Not being a professor, he might never have been able to publish these papers otherwise.

In a way, the fact that he worked at the Patent Office rather than at a university made it easier for Einstein to be so radical with his

Mileva, Hans Albert, and Albert.
Courtesy of the Leo Baeck Institute, New York (F 5373M)

theories. Imagine how difficult it would be for a physics professor to write a paper that contradicted what was being taught at his or her university. Would that put the professor's job or reputation at risk?

In May 1905 Einstein wrote a letter to Conrad Habicht, his old friend from the Olympia Academy, detailing the paper he intended to write:

I promise you four papers ... the first of which ... deals with radiation and the energetic properties of light and is very revolutionary. ... The second paper is a determination of the true sizes of atoms. ... The third proves that ... bodies on the order of a magnitude of 1/1000 mm, when suspended in liquids, must already have an observable random movement. ... The fourth paper is only a rough draft at this point, and is about the electrodynamics of moving bodies that employs a modified theory of space and time.

Einstein never told Habicht about the fifth paper. Perhaps Einstein didn't know at the time that he would write it. Yet his final paper led to his most famous equation: $E = mc^2$.

Looking back on his Miracle Year, Einstein told his colleague Leó Szilárd, "They were the happiest years of my life. Nobody expected me to lay golden eggs." Einstein laid the first golden egg three days after his 26th birthday.

The First Paper: Light Is a Wave *and* a Particle

Scientists had long theorized about the true nature of light. (When physicists talk about "light" they're using the word as shorthand for "electromagnetic radiation," which includes not only the light you see but also radio waves, X-rays, microwaves, and so on.) Most believed light was a wave, transmitting its energy the way an ocean wave transmits its energy: in regular, continuous, up-and-down movements called oscillations. Still others, the first of whom was Isaac Newton, believed that light was a stream of particles, transmitting its energy in small "packets," like falling rain.

Einstein had a revolutionary idea: light was both a wave *and* a particle. Both of the main theories on light had their strengths, but they also had their weaknesses. Einstein came up with a way to pull out the strengths of each theory to answer the weaknesses of the other.

Light certainly behaves in many ways like a wave. It reflects—bounces—the same way a ripple of water does when it strikes a wall. It also diffracts—or bends—when it passes the edge of a solid object.

The Einsteins lived in this apartment when Hans Albert was born and when Albert wrote his "Miracle Year" papers. Today it is a museum.
Courtesy Einstein Haus, Bern

Max Planck (1858–1947)

If Albert Einstein had a professional father figure, it was Max Planck. When Einstein sent his papers to the *Annalen der Physik*, they ended up on Planck's desk. He edited the journal. The German physicist did not always agree with Einstein's theories, but he believed competing ideas should be discussed, so he published every one of Einstein's papers.

Though Einstein's first 1905 paper supported Planck's groundbreaking work on light quanta,

Planck himself did not accept the new theory until the 1911 Solvay Conference—after Einstein had a chance to talk to him. "I largely succeeded in convincing Planck that my conception [of light quanta] is correct, after he has struggled against it for so many years," Einstein wrote a friend. Both Planck and Einstein were skeptical of quantum mechanics in their later years, which was ironic since they were the two scientists most responsible for the birth of the field.

Planck was secretary of the Royal Prussian Academy of Sciences in 1914 when he persuaded Einstein to move to Berlin (see page 59). Planck lived in Germany throughout both world wars, but he died shortly after the second conflict ended.

Max Planck. Library of Congress Prints and Photographs Division (LC-B2-1250-11)

But most of all, for the wave theory, when two light beams intersect, they combine. Take a look at a lake or an ocean on a windy day. Do you notice that when two waves run into one another a larger wave pops up for just a moment? And just as quickly, the water level can drop down, way down? Light does that, too. However, you can't see it happening around you because light is traveling so fast and in so many directions, it all looks the same. But in a laboratory, scientists can force light to shine in one specific direction, and when two of these beams are brought together they can create bright and dark bands, called an interference pattern. When the peaks of two light waves combine, they create a brighter line, but when a peak and a valley combine, they cancel each other out and create a dark line.

But physicists learned light behaved in other ways, and not like a wave at all. In 1900 Max Planck was trying to explain why, when light struck certain metals, the metal gave off electrons. The math to explain this didn't work if he used the popular wave theory. But if he thought of the light as being bundled up in small packets, which he called "quanta" (the plural of "quantum"), he could explain it.

Planck was just trying to explain what he was seeing in the laboratory. He had come up with a math trick, one that he admitted privately was "an act of despair." He wasn't necessarily saying that light *was* a bunch of packets. In 1905, however, Einstein did say that.

Einstein's paper convinced few scientists, including Planck. Most clung tightly to the wave theory. But Einstein had suggested that his theory could be verified through experimentation. It wasn't until 1916 that Robert Millikan, while trying to *disprove* it, confirmed Einstein's theory about the photoelectric effect. Then in 1923, Arthur Compton proved the existence of light quanta, which in 1926 Gilbert Lewis began calling "photons."

The Second Paper: The Size of Atoms

A MONTH and a half after Einstein completed his photoelectric effect paper, he finished another, this one calculating the rough size of atoms and simple molecules. Scientists at the time were still unsure that atoms even existed, and Einstein claimed he had determined their size!

The idea that the world was made up of atoms had been around since the ancient Greeks. But what were atoms? It was a little like saying "elephants exist" without knowing how big they were or knowing they had trunks. Without an actual elephant, a photo, or at the very least a footprint, how could you be sure?

The Photoelectric Effect

EINSTEIN'S WORK on the photoelectric effect had more to do with the nature of light than it did the practical applications of his theory. That would come in time. Today you can easily find solar cells being used to convert light energy into electricity.

You'll Need
➤ Sticky notes
➤ Calculator with a solar cell

In this activity you will be testing a solar cell under several conditions. To begin, pull 10 to 15 sticky notes off a pad, keeping them together. There should be enough notes in the pad to block out sunlight when placed over a solar cell.

Turn on a solar calculator outside, on a sunny day. Punch in several numbers so that you can clearly read the display. Now place the pad of sticky notes over half of the solar cell. Wait a few moments—do the numbers in the display fade

out? If not, cover slightly more of the solar cell, little by little, until the numbers fade away. If the numbers faded out when half the cell was covered, slowly *uncover* the solar cell until they reappear.

How much of the calculator's solar cell was needed to power it in direct sunlight?

Now move inside, away from any windows, where the only light comes from artificial sources—lightbulbs. Repeat the process of covering the solar cell with the pad of sticky notes until you can determine how much of the cell is needed indoors.

Compare your results, indoor to outdoor. What can you say about the energy contained in sunlight compared to artificial light? Can you think of other ways to use a solar cell to test different types of light? How do compact fluorescent bulbs compare to incandescent bulbs? How much light energy is blocked out on a cloudy day? How dim can a room be and have your calculator still work?

The answer was in a solution of sugar water, Einstein wrote. When sugar is added to water, the solution's viscosity changes. Viscosity is just another way of saying how easy (or not) it is to move through a liquid—its "stickiness." Tar is very viscous. Water is not. When sugar is added to water it becomes more viscous—the more sugar that is added, the more viscous the water becomes. Compare maple syrup, which is essentially thick sugar water, to a glass of water and you'll get a good idea.

But what does viscosity have to do with the *size* of sugar molecules? Imagine a ball pit filled with children. The small balls are water molecules and the much larger kids are sugar molecules. The more children in the ball pit the more difficult it would be for you, a "sugar molecule," to move from one side to the other. By comparing how fast you could move through a ball pit with 10 children to moving through a pit filled with 30 children you could, with some fancy mathematics, determine how big those kids really are.

Einstein's paper was backed up with experimental data that other scientists could confirm. Using this data he calculated the diameter of a sugar molecule to be 0.000000099 cm. It turns out he was absolutely correct.

In addition to submitting this paper to the *Annalen der Physik*, Einstein sent it to the University of Zurich as his doctoral dissertation. At the time the Poly did not grant PhDs, but the university did. When professor Alfred Kleiner first saw Einstein's paper he rejected it. Too short, he said. Einstein then added a clarification, a single sentence, and resubmitted it. This time it was accepted. In August 1905 he became Dr. Einstein.

Like children in a ball pit, Einstein determined the size of sugar molecules dissolved in water.

The Third Paper: Atoms Exist

TEN DAYS after Einstein submitted his paper on the size of atoms, he finished another paper proving that atoms actually exist. In this paper Einstein didn't pull a theory seemingly out of thin air; he used the well-known (but at the time mysterious) phenomenon known as Brownian motion to explain his reasoning.

Brownian motion comes from observations made by English botanist Robert Brown. In 1828 he noticed that when tiny grains of pollen were suspended in a liquid and observed under a microscope, they appeared to move. They didn't seem to move in any regular pattern, however, but would jump around in a random zigzag. To show that they were not moving under their own power, that they were not somehow alive, Brown repeated his experiments with small particles of sand, glass, and metal, and they all moved as well. Something other than the particles themselves must be responsible. But what?

Einstein wrote that it was atoms or molecules in the seemingly motionless liquid that were pushing the solid particles around. In his view, atoms were constantly in motion, bouncing off one another. Every so often an atom that was moving particularly fast, or a group of atoms that just happened to be moving in the same direction, would bang into the particle and cause it to move.

Imagine for a second that you are standing in the center of a closed room. With you are 40 other people, and each of them is moving around in a different direction. Some are walking and some are running, and you are all blindfolded. If one of those people were to bump into you, you would move. Because you could never be sure from which direction somebody might hit you, your movement would be random. You would zigzag.

Statistics—probability—was the key to Einstein's argument. The random jumps of Brownian motion showed that the atoms surrounding the particle were bouncing around in every direction. By estimating the mass of these atoms and the speed at which they were likely moving, he could determine how much "push" each would have in a collision. Measure the distance the particle actually did move, and you could confirm his theory.

Einstein could determine the kinetic (motion) energy of atoms or molecules in a liquid using thermodynamics. It is a complicated subject, but Einstein was able to calculate that a small solid particle, 0.0001 mm in diameter, should rattle 0.006 mm side-to-side over one minute in water at room temperature. And then he finished: "Let us hope that a researcher will soon succeed in solving the problem posed here, which is of such importance in the theory of heat." In other words, "I've given you the

Michele Besso and Anna Winteler in 1898, shortly after being married.
Besso Family, courtesy AIP Emilio Segre Visual Archives

answer—let somebody else confirm it with an experiment."

And somebody did. In 1908 the French physicist Jean Baptiste Perrin came up with a way to check Einstein's numbers. "Right from the first experiment," he wrote, "it became manifest . . . that the displacements verified at least approximate the equation of Einstein."

In 1949, physicist Max Born looked back at what Einstein had written. "[It] did more than any other work to convince physicists of the reality of atoms and molecules, of the kinetic theory of heat, and of the fundamental part of probability in the natural laws."

The Fourth Paper: Special Relativity

THE FOURTH paper Einstein submitted to the *Annalen der Physik* in 1905 was titled "On the Electrodynamics of Moving Bodies." It is better known today as the Special Theory of Relativity. It caused nothing short of a revolution in physics, and it even seemed to run against common sense.

Einstein hadn't even finalized his thinking about this topic until five weeks before he turned in the paper. He told Besso that he was about to give up on his theory, but one morning he showed up at his friend's door and said, "Thank you. I've completely solved the problem." Something Besso said had triggered his brain, and the answer came to Einstein in his sleep. After five weeks of writing and rewriting, he turned his paper over to Mileva to check the math while he took to his bed to rest—for two weeks.

While the theory was complicated, the basic idea was not. More than two hundred years earlier, Newton had outlined his own laws regarding motion (see page 7). All Einstein said was that the same sort of laws applied to light as to physical objects.

According to Newtonian physics, if you are riding on a train with the curtains drawn (and it's a very smooth train), there would be no way for you to tell that you were in motion. Toss a ball in the air and it would fall to the floor inside the train the same way it would if you tossed it in the air while standing alongside the track.

Einstein now claimed that you wouldn't be able to run an experiment on the train using *light* that would show you were in motion. Light on the train would move at 186,000 miles per second, and light standing alongside the track would move at the same speed.

But wait a second... wouldn't the light on the train move *faster*, at least to the person standing beside the track outside? If the person inside the train threw a ball forward with a speed of 30 mph, and the train was moving at 50 mph, wouldn't a person beside the tracks see it moving 80 mph—30 + 50?

The Michelson-Morley Experiment (1887)

The Michelson-Morley experiment is considered to be one of the greatest "failed" experiments in the history of physics. For years scientists believed that light was a wave. Just as an ocean wave travels through water and a sound wave travels through air, physicists felt a light wave must travel through *something*, called a medium.

But what was that medium? They couldn't see or touch it, but they knew it had to exist. *Everywhere*. It had to be rigid, because light traveled so quickly through it, but not affect anything else moving through it—you, me, your dog. And they gave it a name: ether.

American scientists Albert Michelson and Edward Morley came up with an experiment to determine if the ether existed. First, they knew that if the ether existed, the Earth had to be flying through it as the Earth revolved around the sun. If they could compare the speed of light beams shined in different directions on Earth as the planet moved through the ether (at about 18 miles per second), and those speeds were different, it would strongly support that the ether exists. Think of a boat traveling through the medium of ocean water—if the boat sails in the same direction as the waves, the waves would strike it less often (more slowly) than if the boat was sailing across the waves.

Michelson and Morley built a device that divided a single beam of light into two parts, bounced the two beams at right angles (perpendicular) to each other using mirrors, then rebounded them back to the same point. If these two beams, which had traveled in different directions through the ether, were then compared and their speeds were found to be different, it had to be caused by the Earth moving through the ether.

But the light beams' speeds weren't different. No matter how many times they tried the experiment, the two beams appeared to return at the same moment. The scientists assumed they had made an error, not because of their results but because they still believed that ether existed. It had to! Every other scientist in the late 1800s thought so as well.

Years later, when Einstein's Special Theory of Relativity began to be accepted, physicists looked back at the Michelson-Morley experiment as a misunderstood success.

The Speed of Light

BELIEVE IT or not, you can calculate the speed of light in your kitchen.

You'll Need
➤ Microwave oven
➤ 2 paper plates
➤ Large chocolate bar, longer than 5 inches
➤ Ruler
➤ Calculator or computer

The food in your microwave is heated by electromagnetic radiation—microwaves. Like every

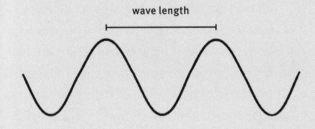

wave length

form of light, microwaves have a wavelength. It's the distance measured between two peaks.

You can find this wavelength by measuring where the peaks melt a chocolate bar. Start this experiment by removing the spinning plate from inside your oven. Place a paper plate upside down over the center spinner. This will keep the chocolate bar from turning.

Unwrap a large chocolate bar, place it on another paper plate, and put the plate face up on top of the first one.

Turn the oven on high for 25 seconds. When you pull the chocolate out, you should see two melted points on the bar. With a ruler, measure the distance between these peaks in inches. Compare it to the number written upside down below.

Now look at the back of the microwave (or sometimes the edge of the door) for the oven's microwave frequency. For most ovens, it will be 2.45

GHz, which means that the wave goes through 2,450,000,000 up-and-down cycles every second. With a calculator or computer (better, since some calculators won't take numbers this high), multiply this big number by the wavelength in inches. This will give you the number of *inches* the microwave travels in one second.

To convert the number of inches into miles, first divide the number of inches you found by 12. This will give you the number of *feet* the wave travels (since there are 12 inches in every foot). Next, divide your new answer by 5,280 since there are that many feet in a mile. Your answer will be the number of *miles* the wave travels in a second.

How close was your calculation to 186,000 miles per second? Can you think of a way to improve this experiment in future tests?

Answer: *Most microwaves should measure 4.8 inches—or about 4³/₄ on a ruler.*

In the same way, if a person inside a very fast train shined a flashlight toward the front of the train, the light would move away from the flashlight at 186,000 miles per second. But if the train (with the flashlight) was moving at, say, 50,000 miles per second, wouldn't somebody alongside the track see the light moving forward at 236,000 miles per second—186,000 + 50,000?

Einstein said no. The speed of light is constant *no matter where you observe it*. In other words, the famous Michelson-Morley experiment (see sidebar) wasn't a failure. They had proven a fundamental aspect of nature, but they just didn't realize it: the speed of light is constant.

Einstein's theory is explained in greater detail in the next chapter. For the time being, think of what it must have been like for Einstein to say that the scientific community was all wrong. He, sitting at his desk in the patent office, had come up with the right answer.

The paper was 31 pages long and contained no reference notes or supporting data. However, he did finish with a "thank you" to his friend Michele Besso: "In conclusion, let me note that my friend and colleague M. Besso steadfastly stood by me in my work on the problem discussed here, and that I am indebted to him for several valuable suggestions."

The Fifth Paper: E = mc²

THE LAST paper Einstein sent to the *Annalen der Physik* in 1905 had to do with mass and energy. Just as Faraday had taken magnetism and electricity, then thought to be separate things, and joined them through a central theory, Einstein described the relationship between energy and mass.

Physicists had only recently discovered radioactivity, and it was not very well understood. How could the element of radium generate so much energy all by itself? While Einstein did not specifically answer this question in his three-page paper, his energy-to-mass conversion formula would eventually be used to explain it.

Einstein's formula came directly from his Special Theory of Relativity. As he fiddled with the equations he'd just come up with, Einstein noticed that they said something new about the nature of matter. As he wrote in his paper, "The mass of a body is a measure of its energy content." Energy and mass weren't just related, they were different forms of the *same thing*! And he had a formula for it.

m = L/V²?

When Einstein first came up with his equation, he did not write it as $E = mc^2$. Instead, it was $m = L/V^2$. The letter m was always used by scientists to denote mass, but he didn't use E to denote energy until 1912. Before that, he used L. He also changed the term V for the velocity (speed) of light to c. The letter c was chosen because it was short for *celeritas*, the Latin word for "swiftness." If you know a little algebra, you can change his new formula with the new terms, $m = E/c^2$, into the one everyone recognizes today: $E = mc^2$.

E = mc²

It can be difficult to imagine, just by looking at Einstein's famous equation, how much energy a certain amount of mass would become if converted entirely into energy. But with a little math and a kitchen scale, you can measure out how much mass it would take to power the city of New York for a year.

You'll Need
➤ Calculator
➤ Kitchen scale with metric units

First, two pieces of information:

✧ According to Einstein's formula, 1 kilogram of mass is equivalent to 25 billion kilowatt-hours of energy.

✧ According to ConEdison, New York City and neighboring Westchester County—approximately 8.4 million people—used about 60 billion kilowatt-hours of electrical energy in the year 2010.

Use a calculator to figure out how many kilograms New York City would need to power itself for one year. (The answer is below.)

Now use a kitchen scale to measure out this mass. If you do not have a scale, look through your kitchen cabinets and you should find a common baking ingredient that is sold in a package that weighs about the same—check the labels.

Are you shocked?

Answer: 60 billion kWh ÷ 25 billion kWh/kilogram = 2.4 kilograms. It is equivalent to about 5.3 pounds, a little more than a standard sack of sugar or flour.

What he found surprised him, and he wrote another letter to Habicht. "The contemplation is amusing and attractive, but I don't know if the good Lord is laughing at it and leading me around by the nose."

Throughout his career, Einstein loved to find simple, elegant solutions to what seemed to be very complicated questions. The fact that the relationship between mass and energy appeared so simple convinced him that it must be correct.

As with his paper on Brownian motion, Einstein suggested a way to show that his theory was correct. The answer could be found in "bodies whose energy content is variable to a high degree (e.g. with salts of radium)." He calculated that if 226 grams of radium was allowed to sit for one year releasing radioactive energy, which was created by minute amounts of mass converting into energy, that radium would decrease in mass by 0.000012 grams. Unfortunately, no laboratory scale at the time was that precise, so there was no way to test the theory.

One thing could be said about Einstein's equation, though: if it was true, a very small amount of mass, when multiplied by the speed of light *twice*, would turn into a *huge* amount of energy. This relationship explained where the sun got all its energy, and it would become the basis of the atomic bomb.

Stuck in the Patent Office

With five revolutionary papers published in one of physics' most prestigious journals, Einstein thought the scientific world would come knocking. What did they think about Special Relativity? "He expected sharp opposition and the severest criticism," his sister, Maja, later wrote. "He was very disappointed. His publication was followed by icy silence. The next few issues of the journal did not mention his paper at all. The professional circles took an attitude of wait and see."

So Einstein waited, too. And wrote. Friedrich Haller promoted him to Technical Expert, Second Class in April 1906 and gave him a raise. Though he may have been frustrated, it was probably good that Einstein remained in Bern, scribbling notes, rather than trying to prepare lectures as a college professor. He authored six more papers in 1906. And in November 1907, Einstein had what he called "the happiest thought of my life":

I was sitting in a chair in the patent office at Bern when all of a sudden a thought occurred to me: If a person falls freely he will not feel his own weight. I was startled. This simple thought had a deep impression on me. It impelled me toward a theory of gravitation.

Einstein was onto something. He called this revelation the Principle of Equivalence, that gravity and acceleration were the exact same thing. This happy thought of a man falling off a building would eventually lead him to the *General* Theory of Relativity. It would describe all types of bodies in motion, not just in a straight line at a constant speed. But for the time being, he wrote. By 1910 he had more than two dozen papers published in various physics journals.

The University of Bern, where Einstein lectured for the first time.

In 1908 Einstein applied for a job as a high school math teacher, but he didn't get it. In fact, he wasn't even one of the three finalists. Then, at the urging of Alfred Kleiner, the dean of physics at the University of Zurich, Einstein applied to be a *privatdozent* at the University of Bern starting in February 1908. A *privatdozent* was a part-time position, the lowest rung on the teaching ladder. Einstein would lecture for any student willing to sign up for (and pay for) his class. Very few students did.

For his first lectures, Einstein had three paying students, and two of them he already knew—Michele Besso and Heinrich Schenk, both of whom worked with him at the patent office. Sometimes his sister, Maja, sat in. She was attending the university at the time. Still, if he wanted to be a professor, he needed to show he could teach.

Kleiner, who was interested in hiring Einstein, attended one of his lectures. Einstein was nervous and disorganized, and only one student sat in. Kleiner went away unimpressed.

3

Special Relativity

1905

WHEN EINSTEIN FIRST wrote about Special Relativity, very few in the scientific community understood it, much less believed it. There were even jokes made about how few scientists did.

This might be the first time you've ever read about his theory in detail, so don't worry if it sounds a little crazy—you are not alone. It took the best minds in physics years to determine that Einstein was correct, so you can cut yourself some slack.

The purpose of this chapter is to let you know what the Special Theory of Relativity says. For the time being, don't worry if you don't *believe* it. Later in this book you'll learn about the experiments that confirmed Einstein's theory.

What's So Special?

You might wonder, why is Special Relativity "special"? In the beginning, Einstein only looked at one type of motion—simple, straight-line motion, like a train rolling along a track. The train didn't shake or turn, brake or accelerate; it just cruised along. If you sat inside this train with its windows covered, you wouldn't even know it was moving. This type of motion was a "special" case. And to be honest, rarely does anything move in this way.

That's right, when Einstein first wrote about relativity he chose the easiest, most basic type of motion possible. (In Chapter 5 you will learn about *General* Relativity, which includes all other types of motion.) He didn't even call it special at the time—that term wasn't used until he started writing about his general theory.

It's Relative

So what does Einstein mean by the term "relativity"? Motion, he said, could only be described by comparing one object *relative to* another. Think again of being inside that train car rolling on the track. Slide back the curtain and you'll see the countryside rolling by— you're moving *relative to* the ground beneath you.

Now it's time for your first thought experiment.

 Moving Through Space

Imagine that you are inside a space capsule—a spherical capsule with no front or back end. Its engines are off, so you are not accelerating. You're far from Earth, so far that you cannot see any planets, stars, or galaxies. Forget how you got there, just image that you are there. Now ask yourself: Are you moving? If so, how could you tell?

Now imagine that you look out the window and see another spherical capsule fly past you. Can you now say that you are moving? Or is it the other spacecraft that is moving? Maybe you're both moving. How do you know?

Einstein stated that all motion is relative. This was not a new thought—Newton said the same. What made Einstein's statement unique was that he said there is not a place of "absolute rest" in the universe.

Many physicists believed that the ether, the mysterious background medium through which light traveled (page 29), defined this state of absolute rest. The universe was a vast ocean of ether. We sailed through the ether, light waves all around.

No, said Einstein. There is no ether. Motion can only be defined when relating two "reference frames" to each other. The first reference frame in the thought experiment above was your space capsule—Capsule A. The second reference frame was the other capsule—Capsule B. When you looked out and saw Capsule B pass by, which capsule was moving?

You may have thought you were sitting still while Capsule B flew by.

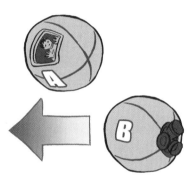

You may have thought Capsule B was still while you, in Capsule A, flew by.

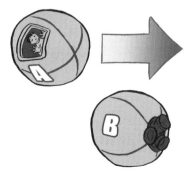

Relative Motion

Y OU DON'T have to go to outer space to do your own observations on relative motion. The next time you take a long car ride on a highway, try this out.

You'll Need
➤ Adult driver
➤ Car with a reclining front seat
➤ Long, smooth highway

This activity works best on an interstate or multilane highway, away from the city. You don't want to be able to see tall buildings, bridges, trees, or streetlights out the car window.

Sit in the passenger seat of a car as it cruises along. Look around. Can you say with certainty which direction you are moving? Be specific in the way you answer the question. You are moving, but *relative to what*?

Keeping your seat belt on, recline your seat all the way so that you are flat on your back. For this to work, you should only be able to see sky out the windows around you, and (on occasion) nearby cars and trucks. No trees, no buildings, no bridges.

Try to ignore the shakes and bumps you feel, and try to forget what you already know—that you're in a car traveling down a highway. Focus only on the nearby vehicles you can see out the windows. Describe the motion of each vehicle you see, and again, describe the motion *relative to you*. Ask yourself these questions:

✧ Based on what you see, if a nearby car moves from the front of your car to the back, is your car moving forward or is the other moving backward?

✧ If another car moves from the back of your car to the front, is your car moving backward or is the other car moving forward?

✧ If another car appears to be sitting beside your car, can you say that you are moving at all?

Or maybe you thought you were both moving.

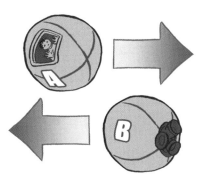

In truth, the best you can say is that Capsule A and Capsule B, two reference frames, are moving *relative to each other*.

As you can see, or imagine in a thought experiment, it is difficult—impossible, actually—to describe motion without using two frames of reference. And as you will soon see, it is also difficult to describe the notion of time.

When Did It Happen?

SUPPOSE YOU are inside your house on a rainy day, looking out your window at the tree in the front yard. Suddenly you see a flash—a bolt of lightning strikes the tree. The next day you tell your friend what you saw, and your friend asks you, "When did it happen?" You remember looking at the clock and say, "It struck at 4:02 PM."

But did it really strike at 4:02 PM, or was that just what you concluded? The lightning struck and you looked at the clock, which read 4:02 PM. The position of the watch's hands and the lightning bolt were *simultaneous*, so you concluded that it struck at that moment.

Einstein would disagree with you. He would say that the perception you had that two events were simultaneous could not be proven. Your perception of *simultaneity* was relative to your frame of reference. In his paper on the Special Theory of Relativity he described a thought experiment to demonstrate why.

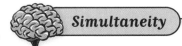 **Simultaneity**

Imagine that you are standing beside a railroad track as a train zips by going very fast. A person is standing in the middle of the train, the same distance from the engine and caboose. Just as the person on the train passes where you are standing, a lightning bolt strikes the ground beside the engine *and* the caboose.

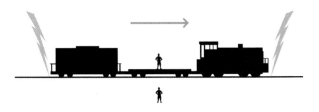

Would you, standing the same distance between the lightning strikes, see the flashes at exactly the same moment? In other words, would the lightning flashes appear to be *simultaneous*?

Now think of the person on the train. Would the lightning strikes appear *simultaneous* to her? Remember, in the time it takes for the light to reach her, the fast train has moved forward some distance.

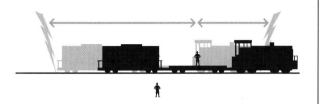

According to Einstein's theory, you and the person on the train could not agree that the lightning bolts struck the ground beside the train at the same moment. Here's why. You, standing an equal distance between the lightning strikes, will see the flashes at the same instant. The speed of light is constant for both flashes, and they go the same distance, so you will see the flashes at the same instant.

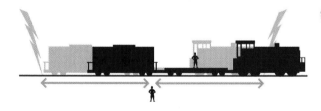

The person riding on the train, however, will not agree with what you observed—she will see the flash at the engine before she sees the flash near the caboose because, in the time it takes for the light to get to her, she has moved closer to the engine flash and farther away from the caboose flash.

Time and Motion

EINSTEIN'S SIMULTANEITY thought experiment showed that it was impossible for two people in two different frames of reference to agree on the concept of time. But it gets even weirder. According to the Special Theory of Relativity, two people in two different reference frames can't agree on how fast time is progressing. One hour for one person is not necessarily the same as one hour for another.

Time Dilation

Imagine a very special type of clock that uses light as its timepiece. In it, a beam of light bounces up and down between two mirrors.

Because the speed of light is constant, and because you can measure the distance between the two mirrors, you could count the number of times the light bounces back and forth between the mirrors as a sort of clock. If the mirrors were 1 mile apart, and a light beam bounced 186,000 times (thereby traveling 186,000 miles), you would know 1 second had passed.

Now imagine you took the light-bouncing clock on a train ride. As you sat in the train with the clock on your lap, no matter how fast the train moved it should operate the same way. To *you*. But how would it look to the person standing beside the track as the train rushed by very fast?

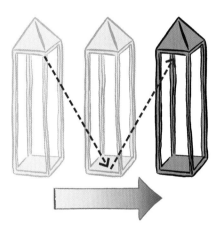

The light leaves the top mirror, but by the time it reaches the bottom, the bottom mirror (on the moving train) has moved forward. After the light bounces off the bottom mirror, but before it reaches the top mirror, the train has moved

forward again. To the person on the train, nothing seems strange. But what would the person standing beside the tracks say about the path the light took?

Einstein looked at the zigzag pattern that would be created by a light-bouncing clock and noticed the different distances the light appeared to travel. For the person on the train, everything seemed normal. One bounce was equal to the distance between the mirrors. But for the person beside the track, the path between bounces was *longer*.

Since the speed of light is the same for both observers—remember, it's constant—more time would go by in a single bounce for the person standing beside the track. In other words, time would go faster for the person standing beside the track than it would for the person on the train . . . when viewed by the person beside the track, of course.

Does that sound strange? Try this:

Time Dilation, Part II

Think back to the Moving Through Space thought experiment. In it you couldn't say which of the spacecraft was moving, only that they were moving *relative to each other*. Now apply that knowledge to the train and the light-bouncing clock. What if the clock was held by the person standing beside the track?

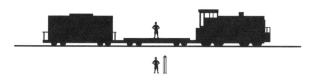

If you were on the train as it zipped past a person holding a light-bouncing clock, what would the path of light look like? Would it appear longer?

As you probably guessed, the light path when viewed from the train would appear longer. And, according to the first Time Dilation thought experiment, time would go faster on the train than it would for the person beside the track *when viewed from the train.*

You might wonder why time would move faster for the observer in both thought experiments. It's simple: time is *relative.* Even though the observer changed, the location of the light-bouncing clock *relative to the observer* was exactly the same.

Consequences

ONCE EINSTEIN determined that *time* appeared to be different from two different frames of reference, he knew that other measurements—distance and mass—would be affected as well.

This is where Einstein's Special Theory of Relativity starts to get into heavy math, calculations that are more complicated than you are familiar with at this point in your school life. Right now it is not important that you be able to follow the math—there are plenty of books that explain his calculations if you're interested (and a math whiz!)—but it is important that you understand *what* his calculations said.

Fast Objects Appear Shorter

In his Special Theory of Relativity, Einstein stated that an object moving very fast, relative to an observer, would appear shorter to that observer than it would if it were standing still (relative to the observer). A train roaring through a station at nearly the speed of light would appear shorter than the same train sitting in a station. He called this "length contraction."

The key word to keep in mind here is "appear," for Einstein wasn't saying that the fast-moving train *was* shorter, only that it *appeared* shorter to the person in the station. And, remembering that all motion is relative, to a person on a fast-moving train the *station* would appear shorter than it would if the train was stopped in the station.

According to Einstein's calculations, an object would appear shorter and shorter the faster it moved, up until the point where it was moving at the speed of light, when its length would be zero. However, Einstein didn't believe this would ever happen, not because an object can't have a length of zero, but because of the way mass behaves as it approaches the speed of light.

Fast Objects Gain Mass

Even stranger than an object getting shorter as it gains speed, Einstein determined that the object would gain mass. That's right, a train flying through a station at close to the speed of light would have more mass than the same train sitting in the station. If you had a scale that could measure the train's mass as it flew by, it would show the mass increasing the faster it went. If it could reach the speed of light, according to the theory of Special Relativity, its mass would be infinite.

Einstein said that this is impossible, that there is a speed limit to the known universe, and that is the speed of light. Of course, there is no possibility of a train, or even a spaceship, getting even close to this speed to test the theory. However, physicists working today with particle accelerators can get parts of atoms to move close to the speed of light, and when they do, these particles gain mass. Einstein was correct.

Time Slows Down as an Object Speeds Up

And finally, as in the Time Dilation thought experiments, as an object speeds up, its internal clock appears to slow down relative to an observer at rest. According to the math, if that object were to reach the speed of light, its time would stop altogether, at least when viewed by a viewer at rest. Einstein claimed that this was one more reason it is impossible for an object to travel at the speed of light.

The Twin Paradox

Imagine a pair of identical twins, each born on the same day. One becomes an astronaut for a mission to a far-off planet. While one twin stays at home on Earth, his brother flies off at nearly the speed of light, reaches the planet, then flies back at the same speed. When they get back together, which twin is older?

This thought experiment was posed to Einstein, and the answer turns out to be far more complicated than it sounds. You might answer that neither twin is older. After all, motion is relative. When the astronaut raced off in his spacecraft, couldn't you just as easily say that the twin on Earth was raced away while the spacecraft stood still? (Remember the Moving Through Space thought experiment?)

Einstein pointed out what some people missed: the astronaut didn't start out at a constant speed, he had to *accelerate* to reach the speed of light. This wasn't a thought experiment about the Special Theory of Relativity, which only dealt with constant, uniform motion. This was a case of acceleration, and he didn't have an answer for this in 1905. He needed to think some more.

Distant Galaxies and the Speed of Light

EINSTEIN DID not use experiments to come up with his Special Theory of Relativity, and because he wrote it more than a century ago, he did not have the same knowledge of the universe that you do. In fact, when he wrote his theory he did not know—nobody knew—that there were other galaxies in the universe. But you, with that knowledge and a simple thought

experiment, can answer the question whether the speed of light is constant, and you don't have to be a Nobel Prize–winning physicist!

 The Speed of Light on Zozon

Imagine that a friend of yours lives on another planet—Zozon—in a different solar system, in a different galaxy, at the farthest point in the universe from our Milky Way. Your friend's galaxy is moving away from the Milky Way (us) at an incredible speed—almost the speed of light.

Now ask yourself these questions:

◆ If your friend is moving away at almost the speed of light (relative to you), would she see things differently on Zozon than you would on Earth? In other words, would visible light behave differently for her than for you?

◆ If you think it would behave differently, would light travel faster or slower on Zozon than on Earth?

◆ Now imagine that her galaxy is racing toward the Milky Way at almost the speed of light. Would that change the way light behaves on Zozon?

◆ If you think light would change because her planet changed direction (relative to you), would her light now travel faster or slower than on Earth?

◆ Finally, imagine that you and your friend never met. She doesn't know if she's moving toward you, away from you, or even if the Milky Way exists. Why does the speed of light on Zozon depend on the speed of our Earth (relative to Zozon)?

As you probably figured out, the answer to the last question is simple: it doesn't. Why would the speed of light on Zozon, or any other planet for that matter, depend on the speed of light on *Earth*? Would planets moving toward Earth have "fast" light, while planets moving away have "slow" light?

The best part of this thought experiment is that you know one thing that Albert Einstein didn't: distant galaxies actually exist. What's more, the farthest galaxies *are* moving away from the Milky Way at almost the speed of light.

When he wrote his Special Theory of Relativity in 1905, Einstein had to imagine trains moving at the speed of light, but as far as he knew, nothing moved that fast. Edwin Hubble didn't discover other galaxies until 1924—more on this in Chapter 6—and later still, other astronomers discovered just how fast the most distant galaxies in the universe are moving. Relative to us, of course.

What You've Learned About Special Relativity

It's time to list what you've learned so far.

✧ The speed of light is constant.

✧ Special Relativity deals only with constant, uniform motion.

✧ All motion is relative. You can only describe motion by comparing two bodies to one another.

✧ It is impossible for two people moving at different speeds to agree whether the same events happened at the same time.

✧ As a fast object moves past an observer, it will appear to be shorter (in the direction of motion) than it would be at rest.

✧ As a fast object moves past an observer, it will appear to have more mass than it would have at rest.

✧ The faster an object moves relative to an observer, the slower time will appear to pass on that object, when viewed by the observer.

Einstein in his Berlin office.
© Underwood & Underwood/Corbis

The Professor Without Socks

1909–1919

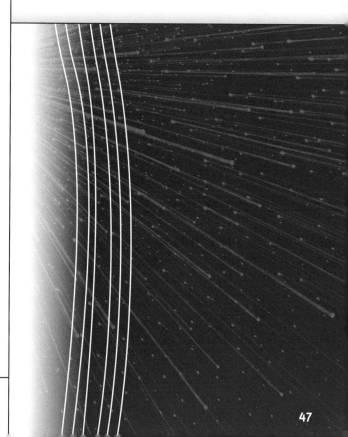

"Truly novel ideas emerge only in one's youth. Later on one becomes more experienced, famous—and foolish."

—Einstein to friend Heinrich Zangger, 1917

FRIEDRICH ADLER WAS insistent. "If it is possible to obtain a man like Einstein for our university, it would be absurd to appoint me," he told the governing board at the University of Zurich. Adler had been offered a position as associate professor, but he really didn't want it. He had worked as Alfred Kleiner's assistant for three years but was more interested in politics than physics.

Adler knew that Einstein was being considered for the same job, and he respected Einstein's genius. When Adler declined the offer, he gave Einstein his big break. In February 1909, Kleiner asked Einstein to become the school's first associate professor of theoretical physics. Though he may have worried about Einstein's teaching style, he hoped Einstein would improve with practice.

Shockingly, Einstein turned down the job. He made more money working at the patent office than the university offered him. He had a family to support. But Kleiner wouldn't take no for an answer twice. He convinced the governing board to match Einstein's salary, and Einstein finally accepted.

A Popular Professor

ALBERT EINSTEIN resigned from his job at the patent office and started teaching at the University of Zurich in October 1909. "I cannot tell you how happy we are because of this change, which will free Albert of his daily eight hours in the office, and he will now be able to devote himself to his beloved science, and *only* science," wrote Mileva to Helene Savić. Mileva was happy as well. She liked Bern, but she loved Zurich.

The Einsteins lived in a second-floor apartment at 10 Moussonstrasse, up the hill from the university. Though they did not have electricity, they did have gas lights, which was an improvement from Bern where Albert wrote by the light of an oil lamp. The apartment, however, had a coal stove that did not always work

Albert Einstein almost died in this apartment when its coal stove malfunctioned.

properly. Once, the stove began putting out deadly carbon monoxide gas while Einstein was asleep on the couch. Luckily his friend Heinrich Zangger stopped by, found Einstein passed out, and dragged him out of the building to safety.

Not long after moving to Zurich, Albert and Mileva learned that she was pregnant with another child. Their second son, Eduard, was born on July 28, 1910. They gave him the nickname Tete. "My dear friends! I am very happy to inform you that the stork has brought us a healthy little boy," Albert wrote to Savić on Mileva's behalf. Yet Eduard wasn't a healthy baby; he would suffer from medical problems his entire life. It had also been a difficult birth, and it took Mileva some time to recover.

Einstein enjoyed his new teaching job. He usually spoke from notes written on scraps of paper and cardboard. Sometimes he would lose a slip or mix them up, so he would tell his students to leave a blank page in their notes, which they would go back and fill in later. "My husband is very happy about his new post," Mileva wrote to Savić. "He much prefers lecturing to the office work in Bern. His audiences are larger than usual and, I discovered in a roundabout way, people like him a lot."

It was true. Despite his disorganization, Einstein's students loved his teaching style. He was different from other professors—he encour-

aged them to ask questions and to challenge him. He made jokes. He would ask if they were following his lecture, and if not, he would try to explain the subject using other examples. And often at the end of his lectures he would ask, "Who's coming to the Café Terrasse?" Here, on the terrace overlooking the Limmat River as it poured into Lake Zurich, they would all enjoy coffee while talking on and on about physics. Or politics. Or philosophy. It was like the Olympia Academy, only larger.

Einstein also didn't look like other professors. His clothes were usually rumpled and his pants were often too short, which only made it more obvious that he rarely wore socks. Most professors dressed for lectures in suits and ties . . . and socks. And his hair? If he owned a comb, he sure didn't seem to use it.

But regardless of his appearance and his strange teaching style, the physics establishment was starting to pay a lot more attention to Einstein. Representatives from German University in Prague contacted Einstein about becoming a professor. It was a step up the professional ladder. But when word got around that Einstein was being lured away from Zurich, the physics students circulated a petition to give him a raise to get him to stay. The university agreed to a 1,000-franc raise and also cut back his lecture schedule to give him more time to work on his theories.

Blue Skies and Red Sunsets

IN ADDITION to all his other accomplishments, in a 1910 paper Einstein explained why the sky is blue. The phenomenon is known as "critical opalescence," which is a fancy way of saying that molecules scatter light. White light is made of all the colors in the rainbow. Blue light has a shorter wavelength than red light, and when it strikes Earth's atmosphere it scatters more than red. In the middle of the day, you see this scattered blue light.

At sunset, the sun's rays must pass through even more of the atmosphere because they are coming in at an angle. So much of the blue scatters away that most of what is left is orange and red.

In this experiment you will re-create the scattering of light as it passes through Earth's atmosphere, creating blue skies during the day and red sunsets near dusk.

You'll Need

- Clear 2-liter bottle
- Water
- Dark room
- Flashlight
- Eyedropper
- Milk

Remove the label from a clear, empty 2-liter bottle. Fill the bottle nearly to the top with water—leave the top 1 inch empty. Screw the cap on tightly. In a dark room, shine a flashlight through the clear water and note the color of the light coming out the other side. It should be the same color, white, as the flashlight by itself.

Remove the cap and add two drops of milk to the bottle. Screw the cap back on and gently shake the bottle until it is all mixed. Shine the light through the bottle from the side. This is the "thin" atmosphere of midday. What color is it now? If the light coming through is still white, continue to add milk, two drops at a time, until it turns blue or bluish. Keep track of the number of drops you add.

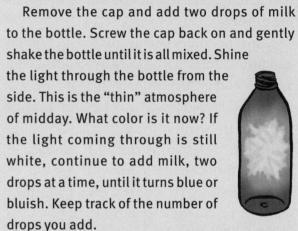

Finally, add the same number of drops you've already added. This will double the number of milk molecules that can scatter the light, creating a "thicker" atmosphere. Now shine the flashlight through this "thick" atmosphere of sunset. What color is the light now?

Prague

DESPITE THE efforts of his students and the university, Einstein eventually accepted the job offer in Prague. There he would be a professor, rather than an associate professor, and would earn twice as much as in Zurich. The university also had an excellent library for Einstein's research. He couldn't refuse.

Einstein's appointment almost didn't happen, however, because he had stated that he was an "unbeliever" on his official forms. All appointments to the university had to be approved by Emperor Franz Joseph, and the emperor insisted that anyone with a government position had to profess a faith—any faith. Einstein had to play up his Jewish heritage, which to him was ethnic rather than religious, to get the job.

Einstein started teaching at German University in April 1911. Mileva was not happy about the move to Prague. She hated Prague. The air was filthy with soot and the water that came out of the tap was brown sludge—the family had to drink bottled water for fear of contracting cholera. Their beds kept getting infested with fleas and bedbugs. The only improvement over Zurich was that for the first time the Einsteins had electric lights.

If the living conditions weren't bad enough, the social life of Prague was also uncomfortable. The city was culturally segregated between ethnic Germans and Czechs. The German minority ruled the city and looked down on the Czechs. Even the University of Prague was divided in half. German University—home of the Institute of Theoretical Physics—was the college Germans attended. Czechs attended Czech University.

Like most of the Jews living in Prague, Einstein was German and was expected to socialize with Germans. But among Germans, Jews were treated as second-class citizens. For Einstein, who had renounced his German citizenship, it felt very awkward. He admitted as much in a letter to Michele Besso: "My position and my institute give me much joy, only the people are so alien to me."

Hans Albert seemed to be the only family member who enjoyed Prague. He loved to go down to the Moldau River to watch the water swirl in eddies as it passed over the locks and spillways. Years later he would become an expert on river sedimentation. Sediments are the small particles of soil that are washed along by moving water but settle to the river bottom as the water slows down.

Einstein had few students. Instead, he was given time to work on his research. It was here that he returned to his quest to develop an expanded theory of relativity, one that included gravitation. One breakthrough he came up with was that light should be affected by gravity.

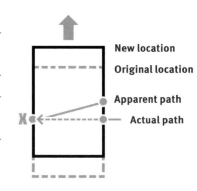

New location

Original location

Apparent path

Actual path

Imagine that you are in an elevator in the middle of space, far from any planet or star that would create a gravitational field. The elevator is attached to a rope that pulls it upward. Since there is no real up or down in space, "up" here refers to the end where your head is in the picture.

inside the eleva-tor, will angle down before hitting the opposite wall. This is because the elevator has moved up a bit before the light reaches the opposite side.

But what if the elevator above is *accelerating* as the light passes through it? What will the person inside see?

Unlike in earlier thought experiments having to do with the Special Theory, this elevator does not move at a constant speed. It accelerates. "Acceleration" is the word used to describe when speed changes. One moment you may be moving at 10 feet per second, but as you accelerate you will later be moving 12 feet per second, then 14 feet per second, then 16 feet per second, and so on.

Now back to the elevator. This elevator has a pinhole in one wall. As it flies through space, somebody shines a light through the pinhole. If the elevator is sitting still, the light beam will eventually strike the opposite wall.

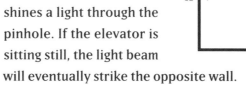

If the elevator is moving at a very fast, *constant* speed, the light beam's path, *when viewed from*

The easiest way to answer this thought experiment (if you can call it easy!) is to break the light's path into four different pieces. The hole, where the light enters, is labeled A. As the light moves toward the opposite wall, it passes through Line 1, then Line 2, Line 3, and finally hits the wall.

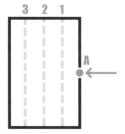

Though an elevator would have to be accelerating *very* quickly to see this happen—remember, light moves at 186,000 miles per second—for the sake of this thought experiment, imagine that light moves slowly enough to see it move across the elevator. When it enters through the hole at A, the elevator is moving 10 miles per second. But by the time it reaches Line 1, the elevator has accelerated to 20 miles per second. So, during the first part of the light beam's journey, the elevator is moving between 10 and 20 miles per second—let's say an average of 15 miles per second. If the elevator is moving at 15 miles per second, the light beam would appear to bend down at an angle (when viewed from inside), hitting Line 1 at Point B.

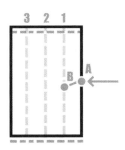

Yes, this is a complicated explanation, but hang in there!

The light beam now leaves Point B, traveling between Line 1 and Line 2. When it leaves Point B, the elevator is moving at 20 miles per second, but by the time it passes Line 2 the elevator has accelerated to 30 miles per second. So, during the second part of its journey the elevator is moving between 20 and 30 miles per second. This time, call it an average of 25 miles per

second—faster than it was moving earlier. This means that for this part of its journey, the light beam's path bends down a little more (when viewed from inside), hitting at Point C.

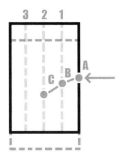

Are you seeing the pattern? Now, when the light travels between Line 2 and Line 3, the elevator accelerates from 30 to 40 miles per second. On average, that's about 35 miles per second—even faster. The light beam's path angles down even more! It passes Line 3 at Point D.

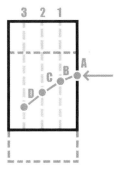

Finally, for the last part of its journey, the elevator accelerates from 40 to 50 miles per second, an average speed of 45 miles per second.

The path angles down even more, and the light beam finally hits the opposite wall.

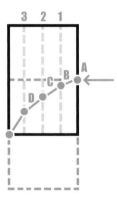

Take a good look at that last picture and the path the light beam traveled. Does it look straight? No. But does it look familiar?

Try a quick experiment: roll a ball off the edge of a flat table. Watch the path it takes to the ground. Try it a few times. What path does it take?

That's right. The path of a ball being pulled downward by gravity is the same sort of path that a beam of light would take if moving through an accelerating elevator. Because Einstein's Principle of Equivalence says that gravity and acceleration are the same thing, a

light beam passing through a gravitational field should behave the same way it would while passing through this accelerating elevator. Gravity should "pull" on light, causing it to bend.

Whew—that was easy!

A thought experiment was one thing, but how could Einstein's theory be tested in reality? Einstein looked to the sun, the most massive object in our solar system, the object with the strongest gravitational pull. If he was correct, light from any distant star should bend as it passed close to the sun's gravitational field. An observer on Earth might be able to determine if the star "moved."

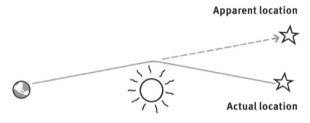

Einstein made the calculations. He predicted that light from a star should bend 0.83 seconds of arc while passing near the sun. (He later found an error and revised his estimate to 1.7 arc-seconds.) A second of arc is a measurement used by astronomers to describe the location of stars. Einstein was saying that the star should *appear* to move a tiny distance—1.7 arc-seconds is about 1/1000 the diameter of the full moon—when it was nearly lined up with the sun. Luckily, astronomers were able to measure this small amount. If only they didn't have to look directly at the sun to do it.

But Einstein figured out how they could take their measurements. On those rare occasions when the moon came between the Earth and the sun—a solar eclipse—the sun's blinding rays would be blocked out just long enough that an astronomer could see the stars surrounding it. Take a photograph, compare it to a photo of the stars when the sun wasn't nearby, and bingo!—you'd have your answer. He published his new idea in 1911, and ended by stating, "It would be a most desirable thing if astronomers would take up the question here raised." After all, there were eclipses every few years.

The first person to take up Einstein's challenge was German astronomer Erwin Freundlich. In 1912 he wrote to Einstein, telling him he wanted to photograph the next suitable eclipse. It was two years away—August 21, 1914—and would best be seen from the Crimean peninsula in the Black Sea. Einstein was enthusiastic, but Freundlich still had plenty of work to do. He had to purchase the proper equipment and find somebody, or some institution, to pay for the expedition.

The idea that gravity could pull on a beam of light the same way it pulled on a ball or any

Bending Light

YOU CAN model gravity's effect on light in your own bedroom.

You'll Need
➤ Adult helper
➤ Large mattress covered in a sheet
➤ Bowling ball
➤ Towel (optional)
➤ Tennis ball (or a similar lightweight ball)

Start this experiment by removing all but the fitted top sheet from the largest bed in your house. For this to work well, the sheet should be tight. A freshly cleaned sheet is best—it will have fewer wrinkles and sags.

With an adult's help, place a bowling ball (or a similar very heavy object) in the center of the bed. This is your sun. (If you are worried about getting the sheet dirty, place a folded towel on the sheet first, just make sure it is tucked tight under the sun.) The heavy sun should push down the center of the mattress.

A tennis ball, or any lightweight ball, will act as your light beam. First, roll it along one edge of the mattress, as far from the sun as possible. Does it change direction as it rolls?

Now try to roll the light beam past the sun, very close but not directly at it. What does the light beam do this time?

Study how the light beam (tennis ball) rolls the closer it gets to the sun (bowling ball). How does this compare to Einstein's eclipse experiment?

other object sounded a little crazy. Even Hans Albert, then only eight, was suspicious. "Father, we are quite alone, nobody can see or hear us," he once said. "Now you can tell me frankly—is this relativity story all bunk?" Einstein laughed. He was happy his son had inherited his skepticism.

Meanwhile, the greatest minds in the scientific community were coming around to the notion that Einstein's theories were not bunk. He was invited to attend the first ever Solvay Conference held in Brussels, Belgium, at the end of October 1911.

There were far bigger names than Einstein invited to the conference—Max Planck, Hendrik Lorentz, Ernest Rutherford, and Marie Curie, to name a few. Each was given 1,000 francs to attend. The topic of the conference

The 1911 Solvay Conference. Nobel Prize winners are in bold. Seated (left to right): **Walther Nernst**, Léon Brillouin, Ernest Solvay, **Hendrik Lorentz**, Emil Warburg, **Jean Baptiste Perrin**, **Wilhelm Wien** (leaning back), **Marie Curie**, Henri Poincaré. Standing (left to right): Robert Goldschmidt, **Max Planck**, Heinrich Rubens, Arnold Sommerfeld, Frederick Lindemann, **Maurice de Broglie**, Martin Knudsen, Friedrich Hasenöhrl, Georges Hostelet, Édouard Herzen, James Jeans, **Ernest Rutherford**, **Heike Kamerlingh Onnes**, **Albert Einstein**, **Paul Langevin.** Photograph by Benjamin Couprie, Institut International de Physique Solvay, courtesy AIP Emilio Segre Visual Archives

was the theory of radiation and quanta. Einstein, the second-youngest attendee, held his own during discussions, but he wasn't the star of the week. Just days after the conference began, Curie learned that she had been awarded the 1911 Nobel Prize for Chemistry for her discovery of radium and polonium.

Not long after returning to Prague, Einstein was contacted about a position at the Poly, recently renamed the Swiss Federal Institute of Technology. The university wanted Einstein to be a professor of theoretical physics, and he quickly accepted. Albert was happy about the offer and Mileva was thrilled. So were their children.

The Solvay Conferences

Ernest Solvay was a Belgian chemist and businessman who made his fortune developing a new process for making baking soda. He was also personally fascinated by science and decided to spend his money gathering the greatest minds to exchange ideas and debate. The first Solvay Conference was held in 1911, and more were held about every three years, except when interrupted by wars. At each conference a main topic was selected, usually the most controversial topic in the fields of physics or chemistry.

Albert Einstein attended four conferences—1911, 1913, 1927, and 1930. The group photo from the first conference has him standing in the back row, with the superstars of physics sitting up front. But by 1927 (page 72), Einstein had earned his front-row seat alongside Marie Curie and Max Planck.

The Solvay Conferences are still held today, though they are now divided by subject, one for physics and another for chemistry. You can learn more about them at www.solvayinstitutes.be.

Back to Zurich

IN THE spring of 1912, before moving back to Zurich, Albert Einstein took a trip to Berlin. Many of his relatives lived in the German capital, including his cousin Elsa Löwenthal. Three years older than Einstein, Löwenthal was a divorced mother of two teenage girls, Margot and Ilse. She was very different from Mileva—outgoing, motherly, and not at all interested in science. But before Einstein left Berlin, he had fallen for her.

The Einsteins returned to Zurich in July 1912. Otto Stern, Albert's assistant from Prague, came along as well. Einstein was determined to crack the riddle of General Relativity, and he needed all the help he could get, particularly with the math. His greatest helper, however, was already working at the Poly. Marcel Grossmann, his former classmate, was now dean of the mathematics department. "You've got to help me or I will go crazy," Einstein begged. Grossmann agreed, on one condition: he wouldn't be responsible for any of the physics.

Grossmann introduced Einstein to a new type of math called tensor calculus, which included a fourth dimension—time—and it was complicated. "Never before in my life have

I troubled myself over anything so much," Einstein wrote that fall. "I have gained enormous respect for mathematics. . . . Compared with this problem, the original theory of relativity is child's play."

Einstein and Grossmann were on the right track. Sometime during his Zurich days Einstein had written the ultimate solution to Gen-

eral Relativity, but he abandoned the approach by mistake. He even started to wonder if he would ever find the solution.

Meanwhile, Einstein tried to ignore the feelings he had for Elsa. But then a birthday letter arrived from Berlin in the spring of 1913. Albert and Elsa began to write to each other regularly, and Mileva suspected trouble. "The situation

Marie Curie (1867–1934)

A brilliant scientist, Marie Curie was the first person to win Nobel Prizes in two different subject areas—physics in 1903 (along with her husband, Pierre) and chemistry in 1911. Born Marie Skłodowska in Poland, she began her college career in Warsaw but moved to Paris in 1891. She graduated from the Sorbonne in 1893 with a degree in physics and a year later earned a degree in mathematics. After being refused a teaching position at Kraków University because she was a woman, she returned to France and a year later married Pierre Curie.

The couple shared a love of science and bicycling. Working together they discovered the radioactive elements radium and polonium in 1898, for which they received the 1903 Nobel Prize for Physics. Marie Curie was the first woman to receive the

Marie Curie. Library of Congress Prints and Photographs Division (LC-DIG-ggbain-07682)

award. Three years later, Pierre was killed when he was run over by a horse-drawn carriage on a Paris street.

Marie Curie met Einstein for the first time at the 1911 Solvay Conference. After the event, Einstein sent her a letter. "I am compelled to tell you how much I have come to admire your intellect, your vitality, and your honesty, and I consider myself fortunate to have made your personal acquaintance in Brussels," he wrote. They continued their professional friendship, and in 1913 their families took a hiking vacation together through Switzerland and Italy.

Curie died of aplastic anemia on July 4, 1934. The illness was caused by years of exposure to the radioactive material in her lab, the health hazards of which were not yet known.

in my house is ghostlier than ever: icy silence," Albert wrote to Elsa. He turned inward, spending less time with his family and devoting even more time to his work.

In August 1913 Erwin Freundlich, who was still planning his eclipse expedition, got married. He managed to convince his new wife to honeymoon near Zurich in September. Yes, they would go sightseeing, but he could also meet Einstein for the first time. The two men immediately hit it off. Einstein tagged along on the newlyweds' day trips, talking all the while about relativity.

Berlin

A YEAR after the Einsteins moved to Zurich, Max Planck and Walther Nernst came to town. They had an offer—a *big* offer. There was a vacancy at the Royal Prussian Academy of Sciences, the most famous scientific body in Europe. If Einstein moved to Berlin, he would be elected to the academy, be given a professorship (but no students, unless he wanted them) at the University of Berlin, and be named director (and for a while the only member) of the Kaiser Wilhelm Institute for Physics.

Einstein asked Planck and Nernst for a day to think about their offer. He suggested that the men take the cog railway up Rigi Mountain to

The Zurich train station, where Einstein met Planck and Nernst with a red rose.

sightsee near Lucerne, and when they returned to Zurich he would meet them at the train station with his answer. If he carried a white rose, he would be declining the offer, but if he carried a red rose, he would be accepting it.

Though his family would be uprooted yet again, Einstein couldn't pass up the chance to be at the center of European physics ... and near Elsa. He met Planck and Nernst with a red rose. "The Germans are gambling on me as they would on a prize-winning hen," he confided to a friend, "But I don't know if I can still lay eggs."

In April 1914 the Einsteins moved to Berlin. Almost immediately, Albert and Mileva's marriage went from bad to worse. In July Mileva moved out of the apartment with the boys, leaving Albert alone. Before the end of the month, Mileva, Hans, and Eduard returned to Zurich. Albert agreed to send half of his salary to Mileva each month as part of their separation agreement.

With his father gone, ten-year-old Hans Albert became the man of the house. "If there was a faucet to fix, a lightbulb to replace, a banister to mend, then he would have to do it," his daughter Evelyn revealed years later. "I think he resented it."

The Great War

AT THE same time that the Einsteins' marriage was collapsing, so were international relations across Europe. On June 28, 1914, Gavrilo Princip shot and killed Archduke Franz Ferdinand and his wife as they rode in an open car through Sarajevo. Ferdinand was an heir to the throne of Austria-Hungary; Princip was a Bosnian Serb. On July 28, the day before Mileva left Germany, Austria-Hungary declared war on Serbia. Two days later Germany mobilized its army and on August 1 declared war on Russia, then France two days later, and on August 4 invaded Belgium on its way to France.

Erwin Freundlich had already headed for the Crimea, loaded with telescopes and cam-

Eduard, Mileva, and Hans Albert Einstein, 1914.
Hebrew University of Jerusalem, Albert Einstein Archives,
courtesy AIP Emilio Segre Visual Archives

eras for the upcoming eclipse. As a German, he now found himself behind enemy lines. Freundlich and his crew were captured by the Russian army and charged as spies. His equipment was seized, and they were sent to a prisoner of war camp. They were traded later for Russian officers who had been imprisoned by Germany.

Einstein's proof would have to wait. "Europe, in her insanity, has started something unbelievable. In such times one realizes to what a sad species of animal one belongs," Einstein wrote to a friend. To his horror, most of his scientific colleagues in Berlin joined the war effort. Fritz Haber, head of the Kaiser Wilhelm Institute for Physical Chemistry, helped develop the deadly weapons—chlorine and mustard gases—used to kill thousands of soldiers during the conflict.

Worse yet, in Einstein's eyes, 93 fellow scientists, scholars, and artists signed a "Manifesto of the Cultured World" backing Germany's military aggression. Einstein refused to sign and might have been labeled a traitor had he not kept his Swiss citizenship. Soon his pacifist friend Georg Nicolai drafted another document. The "Manifesto to Europeans" called for an end to the destructive war. It said, in part, "The struggle raging today can scarcely yield a 'victor'; all nations that participate in it will, in all likelihood, pay an exceedingly high price." Only four scholars signed it, including Nicolai and Einstein.

Hendrick Lorentz (1853–1928)

Dutch physicist Hendrick Lorentz developed the original mathematical approach Einstein used to explore relativity. Lorentz was the first person to come up with a way to explain, using math later called "Lorentz transformations," why the Michelson-Morley experiment did not work. He even said that the length of a rapidly moving object would contract, and so would time. But Lorentz was trying to explain why the ether *had to* exist— Einstein made the jump into saying the ether *did not*, which was a foundation of his Special Theory of Relativity.

Lorentz led the discussions at the first Solvay Conference in 1911 (page 56). Though he and Einstein did not agree on everything, Einstein still admired him. When Lorentz died in 1928, Einstein spoke at his funeral. "I stand at the grave of the greatest and noblest man of our time," he said. "His work and his example will live on as an inspiration."

Einstein also joined the *Bund Neues Vaterland*—the New Fatherland League—a group of pacifists who lobbied German leaders to end the conflict. The group didn't last long, at least officially. It was outlawed in early 1916.

As the war raged on, life became more difficult for the citizens of Berlin. Food was scarce. Meat and sugar were very hard to come by.

Back in Zurich, Mileva and the boys struggled as well. The money Albert sent wasn't enough, so to make ends meet, Mileva taught piano and tutored students in math.

World War I convinced Einstein that he was correct in his support of pacifism.
Library of Congress Prints and Photographs Division
(LC-USZ62-625655)

The General Theory of Relativity

WITH MOST of his colleagues working on the war effort and his family in Switzerland, Einstein spent most of his waking hours focused on relativity. In 1914 he returned to the mathematical approach that he and Grossmann had tried back in 1912 but abandoned. This time it worked.

Einstein knew he was on the right track when he used his new theory to answer a question that had been stumping astronomers for years: the shift in Mercury's orbit. Like other planets, Mercury traveled in an elliptical (oval-shaped) orbit around the sun. But its orbit wobbled. It didn't wobble much, but enough that the point where it was nearest the sun, called the perihelion, moved forward a small amount with every orbit. If you looked at Mercury's path over thousands of years, it would trace out a flower-shaped course. No other planet did this.

The answer to this riddle was in the gravitational effect of the sun. Einstein theorized that the massive body was warping both space and time. Mercury, being the closest planet to the sun, showed this effect the most. Using his new approach to relativity, Einstein calculated how much Mercury's orbit should change: 43 seconds of arc per century. This precisely matched

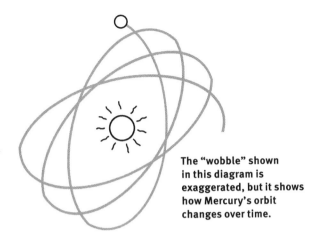

The "wobble" shown in this diagram is exaggerated, but it shows how Mercury's orbit changes over time.

the change astronomers had known for years. Proof at last!

"I was beside myself with ecstasy for a few days," Einstein later wrote. He eventually submitted his findings to the *Annalen der Physik*—they were published in 1916—then sent a letter to Hans Albert, who was then 11 years old. "In the last few days I completed one of the finest papers of my life," he wrote. "When you're older I'll tell you about it."

On November 25, 1915, Einstein presented his Mercury findings in a speech to the Prussian Academy. The General Theory of Relativity took on the concepts of space and time themselves and merged them into what he called space-time. Under his theory, they could not be separated, and space-time determined how large bodies moved through the universe. Gravity was not a force, said Einstein, but the curvature of space-time.

Einstein's announcement did not get the attention it deserved. Many scientists around the world had chosen sides based on their patriotic feelings about the war, which was still being fought across Europe.

Divorce

IN FEBRUARY 1916 Albert Einstein brought up the topic of divorce in a letter to Mileva. She wanted nothing to do with it. She and the boys were struggling in Zurich, but she didn't want to cut off the small security Einstein's support checks brought. The thought of divorce even caused her to fall into a deep depression, and in July she suffered several mild heart attacks. The boys had to live with Albert's old friends the Bessos while she recovered.

Back in Berlin, Einstein wasn't doing much better. He admitted in a letter to Hans Albert that sometimes he was so busy with his work he forgot to feed himself. Food was being rationed in Berlin due to a wartime blockade. In late 1916 he began to lose weight. He shed 56 pounds before collapsing from exhaustion in February 1917. Doctors told him he had a stomach ulcer, and maybe gallstones, too. He was just 38 years old.

Einstein was placed on a special diet, and Elsa began to cook and care for him. In time, he moved into the apartment across the hall from his cousin and her daughters. In October the apartment also became the first office of the Kaiser Wilhelm Institute for Physics. Ilse Einstein worked as Albert's secretary.

The closer Albert grew to Elsa and her daughters, the more he wanted to settle his affairs with Mileva. In early 1918 he again asked her for a divorce, and this time he made a new offer: if he ever received a Nobel Prize, he would turn over the cash award to her. It would be equivalent to about 35 years of the support payments he was then making to her. He also offered to increase his support payments.

Mileva accepted. Because Albert had already been nominated for a Nobel Prize seven times, Mileva rightfully concluded that he would win eventually. It took some time to work out the details of the divorce, but they eventually came to an agreement. And remarkably, Albert and Mileva started to get along again. "I am curious to see what will last longer: the World War or our divorce," he joked in a letter. "They both began essentially at the same time. This situation of ours is still the nicer of the two."

Enter Eddington

THOUGH THEY lived in two countries that were then at war, Albert Einstein and Arthur

Eddington struck up a professional friendship in 1916. They communicated through a mutual friend, astronomer Willem de Sitter, who lived in the neutral country of Holland.

Eddington was an assistant to the Astronomer Royal in Greenwich, England, and was the secretary of the Royal Astronomical Society. He had heard of Einstein's work from de Sitter, and he also learned that Einstein had spoken out against the war. Eddington was a Quaker and held similar ideas about pacifism.

Though Einstein's theories had long been discussed on the European continent, British scientists had mostly ignored him. With the war, some considered his work unworthy of consideration. He was just a German to them. But Eddington was fascinated by the General Theory of Relativity and started working behind the scenes to launch his own eclipse expedition to confirm it.

As the Eddington expedition came closer to reality, the war was coming closer to an end. In the fall of 1918, Germany and its allies began to collapse. Kaiser Wilhelm, the emperor of Germany, fled to Holland and on November 11 an armistice was signed in France. The fighting was over. During the five-year war, more than 15 million had died and 20 million more were injured.

Arthur Eddington.

Proof!

THE 1919 eclipse was rapidly approaching. In order to be sure that he got the photographs he needed, Eddington organized two research groups. He would lead the team headed for Principe, an island off the western coast of Africa. Another team would go to Sobral, Brazil. Hopefully they would have clear skies in at least one of these locations.

While Eddington prepared, Einstein was clearing up his personal affairs. On February 14, 1919, Albert and Mileva were divorced in a Zurich courtroom. Mileva was given custody of the boys. Under the court ruling, Albert was fined 100 francs and ordered not to remarry for two years. But that was in Switzerland. Four months later, on June 2, Albert married Elsa Löwenthal in Berlin. Soon thereafter, he adopted Margot and Ilse.

Eddington sailed for Principe in February and began setting up for the big day. His telescopes and cameras would have to work perfectly to make the journey a success. Even the warmth of sunlight could affect the lenses on his telescopes, causing the photos to blur. If one was even slightly out of focus its image would be worthless. And of course, the sky could be cloudy.

On May 29, Eddington awoke to overcast skies. But the clouds cleared just moments before the eclipse was to begin. The moon blocked out the sun, and the stars of the Taurus constellation shone through as if it were the middle of the night. Eddington took 16 photographs. He telegraphed London: "Through cloud, hopeful."

The team in Sobrol was also lucky. They returned with more than 20 photographs. It took several months for Eddington to analyze all the photos, but by the end of September he felt he had the evidence he needed.

Word got back to Einstein. "Dear Mother," Albert wrote on September 27. "Today I have some happy news. H. A. Lorentz telegraphed

A solar eclipse.

Solar Eclipse

WHAT IS actually happening during a solar eclipse? Make a model to find out!

You'll Need
➤ Adult helper
➤ Table lamp with a removable shade
➤ Large, dark room
➤ Beach ball (or other large ball)
➤ Tennis ball (or other small ball)

This activity is best done at night. With an adult's permission, remove the shade from the table lamp. Put the lamp in the center of a large room and turn it on. This is your sun. Turn off any other lights.

Place a beach ball near a wall, far from the table lamp. The beach ball is Earth. Notice how one side of the ball is lit—the daytime side—while the other is dark—the nighttime side.

Finally, hold a tennis ball between the sun and the Earth, but closer to Earth.

What do you see? Does the shadow of the eclipse cover the entire face of the earth? Does this explain why Eddington had to travel to Africa to see it?

me that the English expeditions have really verified the deflection of light by the sun."

Sir Frank Dyson, the Astronomer Royal (and Eddington's boss), made a formal presentation of Eddington's findings on November 6, 1919, to a joint meeting of the British Royal Society and the Royal Astronomical Society. A packed audience at Burlington House in London learned that the Newtonian universe they had always known was no more. "After a careful study of the plates I am prepared to say that there is no doubt that they confirm Einstein's prediction," Dyson stated.

The next morning the *London Times* headline blared:

REVOLUTION IN SCIENCE
New Theory of the Universe?
NEWTONIAN IDEAS OVERTHROWN

Back in Berlin, Einstein celebrated by ordering himself a new violin.

Planning for an Eclipse

One great thing about solar eclipses is that they are easy to predict, at least for astronomers. If you would like to know about upcoming solar eclipses, visit NASA's eclipse website at http://eclipse.gsfc.nasa.gov/eclipse.html. The next total eclipse that will be visible in North America will occur on August 21, 2017, followed seven years later on April 8, 2024. Mark your calendar!

General Relativity

1915

UNLIKE EINSTEIN'S SPECIAL Theory of Relativity, the General Theory of Relativity was developed over time. Starting in 1907 with the Principle of Equivalence—that acceleration and gravity were the same thing—Einstein began putting together the pieces of the puzzle. This led to his prediction that light should be "bent" by gravity. He published his prediction of how the sun would bend light from distant stars in 1911, and soon Erwin Freundlich was planning his trip to photograph an eclipse.

But it wasn't until 1915 that Einstein figured out the mathematical formula that described his theory. He had worked on the problem for years, admitting to his friend Arnold Sommerfeld in 1912, "Compared with this problem, the original theory of relativity is child's play." Using a complicated type of math called tensor calculus, he finally came up with an answer in 1915:

$$R_{\mu v} - \tfrac{1}{2}g_{\mu v}R = 8\pi T_{\mu v}$$

Looks difficult, right? It is! So difficult, in fact, that we're not going to even discuss the *mathematical* part of Einstein's General Theory in this book. As in the chapter on Special Relativity, we're just going to discuss what the math *says*.

Relativity Review

BEFORE YOU read on, it would be good to review what you've learned so far. You don't realize it, but you've already read about most of the elements of General Relativity.

First, everything in the Special Theory of Relativity is in the General Theory as well. The speed of light is constant. As an object speeds up, relative to another observer, it appears to shorten and gain mass, and time slows down. And it is impossible for two observers in two different reference frames to agree on whether two events were simultaneous or not.

You should also review what you've read about Einstein's early steps toward his theory. The Principle of Equivalence stated that there is no difference between gravity and acceleration (page 33). In 1911, Einstein's thought experiment using the accelerating elevator convinced him that gravity would bend a beam of light in much the same way it would change the path of any mass passing nearby (page 54).

Space-Time

THE CONCEPT of space-time came out of Einstein's prediction that a massive object, such as the sun, would bend the path of light. But it would be wrong, he said, to think of gravity as a force that pulled on light. After all, nothing pulled the light as it bent while passing through the accelerating elevator. And yet it still bent.

No, mass did something weird to the fabric of space and time—space-time. Like the bowling ball sitting on the mattress, the shape of the space around it was warped. A physicist named John Wheeler once described what was going on: "Matter tells space-time how to curve, and curved space tells matter how to move."

Let's take that statement one piece at a time. Think back to the bowling ball experiment. The mattress represented space-time itself. Before you added the ball, it was flat. Anything passing along its surface would move on a direct path. But when you added the large mass (the bowling ball), the surface warped. It curved. The larger the bowling ball, the more it would warp—"matter tells space-time how to curve."

What about the second half of Wheeler's statement? Depending on how the mattress has been warped by the bowling ball, any mass traveling over that curved surface will follow the path created by the warp—"curved space tells matter how to move."

It's a strange way of looking at the universe, where everything does not travel in the straight lines you might expect. That was Einstein's genius, to think of the universe in a whole new way. He later explained what he had done to his son Eduard. "When a blind beetle crawls over the surface of a curved branch, it doesn't notice that the track it has covered is indeed curved," he said. "I was lucky enough to notice what the beetle didn't notice."

Black Holes

ONE OBVIOUS question (at least for physicists) that came from Einstein's theory of space-time was whether it could curve so much that it curved in on itself. Could this happen if the mass was so great that anything passing too close to it, including light, was pulled into it?

Several people, long before Einstein, had already considered this possibility. In 1783 John Mitchell came up with an idea he called the "dark star," one so large that nothing, not even light, could escape. French mathematician

Pierre Laplace made his own calculations in the early 1800s. However, since both men had based their ideas on Newton's particle theory of light, their theories were abandoned when scientists switched over to the wave theory of light.

But it wasn't until 1916, following Einstein's announcement of the General Theory of Relativity, that the subject came up again. Physicist Karl Schwarzchild was an officer in the German army, fighting on the Russian front during World War I. Somehow he found the time to work out how massive, and how small, a star would have to be before it collapsed onto itself. He sent his data to Einstein, who presented it to the Prussian Academy. Sadly, Schwarzchild died from an infection before he could return to Berlin.

Despite the convincing math, Einstein never really believed that these dark stars could exist. Most of the study on this idea was done after he died. American physicist John Wheeler first used the term "black hole" in 1967. Since black holes cannot be seen, the best evidence that they exist is found by studying the behavior of stars near them.

Time and Gravity

EDDINGTON'S ECLIPSE expedition confirmed that the mass of the sun had curved space-time, bending light from distant stars. That explained the "space" (geometry) part of space-time. But what about the "time" part?

The General Theory of Relativity has an explanation for that as well. Einstein calculated that time itself would slow down in a stronger gravitational field when compared to a weaker gravitational field. For example, time would move more slowly on the surface of the sun than it would on the surface of Earth.

Of course, it's rather difficult to measure time's passing on the surface of the sun. Was there another way to confirm the theory? In 1959, researchers at Harvard University compared how a beam of gamma rays affected an atomic reaction at two different places in a campus building, one in the basement (where the beam started) and one in the attic, 74 feet above it. Because the basement was closer to the center of the earth, where the effect of gravity was slightly greater, the reaction there should occur more slowly than the reaction in the attic. And it did!

The Twin Paradox Returns

Do you remember the Twin Paradox thought experiment (page 42) in the chapter on the Special Theory of Relativity? In it, one identical twin rides off to a distant planet and returns at nearly the speed of light, while the other twin stays on Earth. The question was, when they got back together, which twin is older?

Your first reaction would be to say neither. The twin on Earth, when viewed by the twin on the spacecraft, raced away just as fast . . . when viewed by the twin in the spacecraft. Why should either reference frame be special?

According to Einstein's General Theory, the twin in the spacecraft *was* special because he had to accelerate to get up to the speed of light. Remember the accelerating elevator and the Principle of Equivalence? Acceleration is the same thing as gravity, so when the spacecraft raced off, the astronaut twin experienced a strong acceleration to get up to light speed. It would be the same as being in a strong gravitational field . . . where time moves slower.

So, at last, the Twin Paradox has an answer: the twin on Earth would be older. His clock moved faster. If you have ever read any science fiction with space travel written in the last 50 years, you have probably read about a similar situation. Now you know why.

What You've Learned About Special Relativity

It's time to list what you've learned.

✧ Everything in the Special Theory still holds true for the General Theory.

✧ Acceleration is the same thing as gravity. Einstein called this the Principle of Equivalence.

✧ A large mass "bends" space-time. The larger the mass, the more it bends.

✧ If space-time bends in on itself, it becomes a black hole.

✧ Time moves slower in a stronger gravitational field.

The 1927 Solvay Conference. Nobel Prize winners are in bold. Front row (left to right): **Irving Langmuir, Max Planck, Marie Curie, Hendrik Lorentz, Albert Einstein,** Paul Langevin, Charles-Eugène Guye, **Charles Wilson, Owen Richardson.** Middle row (left to right): **Peter Debye,** Martin Knudsen, **William Bragg,** Hendrik Kramers, **Paul Dirac, Arthur Compton, Maurice de Broglie, Max Born, Niels Bohr.** Back row (left to right): Auguste Piccard, **Émile Henriot,** Paul Ehrenfest, Édouard Herzen, Théophile de Donder, **Erwin Schrödinger,** Jules-Émile Verschaffelt, **Wolfgang Pauli, Werner Heisenberg,** Ralph Fowler, Léon Brillouin. Photograph by Benjamin Couprie, Institut International de Physique Solvay, courtesy AIP Emilio Segre Visual Archives

Fame and Persecution

1919–1933

IN ALL HIS years of teaching, Albert Einstein had never experienced anything like it. The students at the University of Berlin were heckling him, disrupting the class and bringing the lecture to a standstill. But it wasn't really Einstein they were mad at, it was all the other people crowded into Auditorium 122.

Almost overnight Einstein had become one of Germany's biggest tourist attractions. Visitors and curious locals came to his lectures to get a look at the professor with wild hair, and his students found it difficult to find a chair to sit in. At first Einstein didn't mind the uninvited guests, but it had gotten out of hand. The school came up with a plan: students who had paid for the course were allowed to take their seats first, and if there was any additional room, others could take the empty seats.

"They cheer me because they all understand me, and they cheer you because nobody understands you."

—Charlie Chaplin to Albert Einstein at the premiere of *City Lights*

Einstein had come a long way from his days as a *privatdozent*, lecturing for the few friends he could talk into attending.

Instant Celebrity

THE ANNOUNCEMENT of Eddington's confirmation of Einstein's theory hit just when the world was looking for something to celebrate. "People were weary of hatred, of killing and international intrigue," wrote physicist Leopold Infeld. "It seemed the beginning of a new era." So many of Europe's great thinkers had turned their talents toward developing creative new ways to kill one another. Now two men from opposite sides of the conflict were trying to explain the very nature of the universe. It certainly helped that neither had been involved with the war effort.

All the attention shocked Einstein. Reporters flooded him with requests for interviews and, as Einstein soon learned, were sometimes more interested in sensationalism than facts. A story in a Berlin paper claimed that Einstein came up with the General Theory of Relativity after seeing a man fall off a building and land safely in pile of "soft garbage," just like Newton came up with the theory of gravity when an apple fell on his head (which also didn't really happen). Einstein wrote to a friend, "The newspaper drivel about me is pathetic."

Elsa stepped into a new role as the gatekeeper at Einstein's office apartment. She would turn away well-wishers and the curious alike. She wasn't just protecting her husband. Albert's mother, Pauline, had been living with Albert's new family since late 1919. She suffered from stomach cancer and was in great pain. Finally, the woman who had taught her son to be independent and to love music died in the Einsteins' apartment on February 20, 1920.

Around this time Einstein was having his own difficulties with Hans Albert. His son announced that he wanted to study engineering. "I think it's a disgusting idea," his father told him. Nevertheless, said 15-year-old Hans Albert, that was what he was going to do. The two argued. It must have reminded Albert of when he had fought with his father after deciding to study physics rather than engineering.

Years later Hans Albert recalled, "He tried to give me advice, but he soon discovered that I was too stubborn and that he was just wasting his time." After graduating from high school, Hans Albert enrolled at the Poly, where he later earned a degree in hydraulic (water) engineering.

While Einstein struggled with his family's issues and his newfound fame, relativity marched ahead without him. "It's so dreadful I can barely breathe anymore," he complained to Max Born. "Not to mention getting around to any sensible work."

During the war Einstein had written a book, *Relativity: The Special and General Theory,* but it had only been published in German. Because of paper shortages, very few copies had been printed. Now there was a bestselling English edition, and others were in the works. (The French edition would be translated by his old friend from the Olympia Academy, Maurice Solovine.) All over the world, physicists lecturing about relativity found themselves speaking to overflow crowds.

But not everyone was a fan of Einstein and the attention he was getting. Right-wing German nationalists blamed the country's defeat on socialists, Jews, pacifists, communists, and everyone else they didn't agree with, and Einstein fit the bill on several accounts. "Einstein's theories [have] been stamped as 'Jewish physics' by colleagues," wrote Born. To some, Einstein's ethnicity was reason enough to dismiss his work altogether.

Worse still, it became common to associate relativity with relativism, the idea that there was no right or wrong, no true or false, no good art or bad art. *Everything* was relative. It was a dishonest charge made by Einstein's critics, but it gained popularity over time. The *New York Times* wrote an editorial titled "Assaulting the Absolute" that suggested that "the foundations of all human thought had been undermined" by relativity.

All human thought? The notion was ridiculous, and Einstein didn't mind saying so. In 1921 he was seated at a banquet beside England's Archbishop of Canterbury. The archbishop asked what relativity had to say about faith and God. "Relativity is a purely scientific matter and has nothing to do with religion," Einstein replied.

International Superstar

IT SOON became clear that Einstein would not be able to hide out in his Berlin apartment forever. Lecture requests flooded in from around the world. He realized that he could use his new fame to draw attention to causes he supported, such as pacifism and Zionism.

In part due to the anti-Semitic rantings of his critics, Einstein had embraced the cause of Zionism. For years—centuries, actually—Jews had been persecuted across the globe. Zionism was a movement to establish a Jewish homeland.

Chaim Weizmann, a British citizen who was president of the World Zionist Organization, convinced Einstein to tour the United States to raise money to establish Hebrew University in Jerusalem. "There is nothing in me that can be described as a 'Jewish faith,'" Einstein admitted. "However, I am happy to be a member of the Jewish people." The tour was set.

On March 21, 1921, the Einsteins set sail for America on the SS *Rotterdam*. Two weeks later, on April 2, they arrived in New York City.

Before they even got off the ship they were swarmed by reporters and photographers. A journalist asked Einstein to sum up his theory in one sentence. "All of my life I have been trying to get it into one book," he laughed, pointing at the reporter, "and *he* wants me to get it into one sentence!" The reporters loved it.

Albert tucked his violin case under his arm and he and Elsa headed ashore. They were greeted by thousands in Battery Park, including the mayor of New York (with a key to the city) and a fife and drum corps playing "The Star-Spangled Banner." Einstein rode in an open car through the crowded Jewish neighborhoods of lower Manhattan on the way to his hotel. There he met his old family friend, Max Talmud, who had immigrated to the United States and changed his last name to Talmey. Later in the week, after a visit to city hall, "he was lifted onto the shoulders of his colleagues and into the automobile, which passed in triumphal procession through a mass of waving banners and a roar of cheering voices."

The American public ate it up. From what they could see, Einstein was witty, kindhearted, and humble. His goofy hair and absentminded

Elsa and Albert Einstein aboard the SS *Rotterdam*.
© Bettmann/Corbis

behavior (or at least the rumors of it) made them like him even more.

Three weeks later he traveled to Washington, DC, where President Warren Harding invited him to the White House. While Einstein and Harding posed for photos, a reporter asked the president if he understood relativity. He admitted he did not. Neither did the US Senate, but that didn't stop them from debating the subject that day in the Capitol building.

The Einsteins eventually traveled as far as Chicago, then returned to the East Coast where Albert lectured for a week at Princeton, New Jersey, his future home. From there he went to Boston, where he spoke at Harvard, and then Hartford, Connecticut. Finally he traveled to Cleveland, Ohio, and Case Western Reserve where the Michelson-Morley experiment had been performed 35 years earlier. There he met with physicist Dayton Miller, who claimed to have found the mysterious ether at last. Were he correct, Miller would disprove relativity, and Einstein wanted to hear what he had to say. He encouraged Miller to keep trying but still felt confident that his theory would hold up. (Miller's work turned out to be incorrect.)

Though the trip had been intended to be a fund-raiser for Hebrew University, it did not raise as much money as Weizmann had hoped. It did, however, raise enough money to establish a medical faculty.

The Nobel Prize for Physics

By now most people, even those not involved in science, believed that Albert Einstein was at the top of the list for the next Nobel Prize for physics. But not if Philipp Lenard had anything to say about it.

Lenard was a German physicist who had received the Nobel Prize in 1905. When Einstein first started corresponding with him in 1905, the pair had been friendly. But the war changed Lenard, and he joined the crowd calling relativity a Jewish conspiracy to undermine German science.

On August 24, 1920, a nationalist organization called the Study Group of German Natural Philosophers held a mass meeting at the Berlin Philharmonic Hall to discuss how to combat relativity. Lenard did not attend, but, to everyone's surprise, Einstein showed up with his friend Walther Nernst. He sat in the audience, taking notes, and when somebody on the stage said something ignorant he laughed out loud.

Three days later Einstein responded to the rally in a Berlin newspaper. He refuted what had been said, then went after the scientist who had supported the event. "[Lenard's] objections to the general theory of relativity are so superficial that I had not determined it necessary until now to reply to them in detail," he wrote. He then picked apart Lenard's objections to relativity, piece by piece.

Furious, Lenard used his influence with the Nobel Prize committee to see that Einstein would not receive the award. The 1920 prize went to Charles Guillaume "in recognition of the service he has rendered to precision measurements in physics by his discovery of anomalies in nickel-steel alloys." The following year then came and passed, but the committee did not hand out a 1921 prize for physics.

This was the last straw for many in the scientific community. They had sat back while Lenard and others bullied the committee into ignoring Einstein. There was now growing pressure to see Einstein honored. The Nobel Prize in 1922 went to Niels Bohr for his work on uncovering the structure of atoms. And, at the same time, the committee announced it would be giving Einstein the *1921* prize for his groundbreaking work on the photoelectric effect.

Philipp Lenard was outraged. He'd received the Nobel Prize for his work on cathode rays, but he was a pioneering researcher on the photoelectric effect. However, he had not *explained* the effect, but had only conducted experiments to *describe* it. Einstein had based his 1905 paper, in part, on observations made by Lenard.

Einstein learned about the award while he was headed for Japan. That fall he and Elsa had embarked on a lecture tour through Asia, including stops in Ceylon, Hong Kong, Singapore, and China. They were not able to return to Europe in time for the award ceremony, so the German ambassador accepted it on Einstein's behalf.

As he had agreed to in his divorce settlement, Einstein turned over the 121,572-kroner cash prize—equal to $32,500 in 1920, or just over $400,000 in 2010 dollars—to his former wife. Mileva Marić Einstein used the money to buy three apartment buildings in Zurich. She lived in one with her sons and rented out the others as her income.

Alfred Nobel and the Nobel Prizes

Every year the Royal Swedish Academy of Sciences announces its highest honors, the Nobel Prizes for physics, chemistry, medicine, literature, economics, and peace. The prizes are the legacy of Alfred Nobel, who invented dynamite in 1866. Nobel was a talented Swedish chemist who intended the explosive to be used to quarry rocks and blast railroad tunnels. But, much to his horror, it was used more in war than for industry.

Alfred Nobel became a very rich man from dynamite and his other inventions. He received 355 patents during his lifetime. But he never married and had no children, and as he grew old he decided that his fortune should be used to honor those who had made great contributions to society. He died in 1896, and his fortune was turned over to the Swedish Academy for this purpose. Five years later, in 1901, the first Nobel Prizes were awarded.

Each winner of the Nobel Prize receives not only a medal but a cash award to continue his, her, or their work. Some of its most famous recipients include John Steinbeck, Martin Luther King Jr., Mother Teresa, Barack Obama, and Doctors Without Borders. You can find information on all who have received it at www.nobelprize.org.

Albert Einstein would never receive a Nobel Prize for relativity.

A Unified Field Theory

In the mid-1920s Albert Einstein became increasingly obsessed with developing a Unified Field Theory. His work on relativity had already linked energy and matter. Could he do the same with gravitation and quantum mechanics? In his heart he believed that he could bring them all together under one set of equations. He published his first paper on the subject in 1929, a paper he later admitted had faults. The search for a Unified Field Theory was a quest he would pursue for the rest of his life.

At the same time Einstein set off on his intellectual journey, the physics community was headed in another direction. Quantum mechanics, the study of the inner workings of atoms, was the hot new field in physics. Einstein had launched quantum theory with his groundbreaking 1905 paper on the photoelectric effect. But as other physicists learned more and more about the quantum nature of the atom, Einstein withdrew.

Probability—chance—was central to quantum mechanics. Werner Heisenberg theorized that it was impossible to determine the exact location of electrons and subatomic particles in an atom. When electromagnetic radiation (light) struck an atom, there was no way to know for sure when, and in which direction, the atom would throw off an electron. It was an educated guess at best. And Einstein refused to believe that nature did not follow rules.

To his credit, Einstein listened to his fellow scientists. He just wasn't buying the whole idea. At the 1927 Solvay Conference, only Max Planck and Hendrik Lorentz joined Einstein as he debated Niels Bohr, the champion of the new science. Over several days Einstein came up with one thought experiment after another, each challenging an element of quantum theory. Each time, Bohr came up with an answer that shot down Einstein's objections. By the end of the week, more of the Solvay's attendees sided with Bohr than with Einstein.

It would be wrong to conclude that Einstein and Bohr, even though they strongly disagreed, didn't admire one another. Bohr credited Einstein with helping him clarify his thinking and to make better arguments for the quantum theory. For his part, Einstein would not have spent as much time debating Bohr if he did not think he was a worthy adversary. Even when they argued, they enjoyed it and would joke around. In a famous exchange, Einstein dismissed the idea of probability by saying, "God does not play dice with the universe." Bohr shot back, "Stop telling God what to do!"

Niels Bohr.
Library of Congress Prints and Photographs Division (LC-B2-5894-8)

Still, it seemed to many that physics might be racing on ahead of Einstein, who was trapped by his own stubbornness.

Niels Bohr (1885–1962)

In 1913 Danish physicist Niels Bohr confirmed Ernest Rutherford's model of the hydrogen atom—an electron orbiting a central nucleus. For this he would receive the 1922 Nobel Prize for Physics. He was also one of the pioneers of quantum mechanics. The arguments between Bohr and Einstein, who didn't believe quantum theory, are some of the most famous debates in the history of physics. Though Einstein lost the debate, he always respected Bohr and the pair had a close professional friendship.

Bohr was in Denmark when the Germans invaded in 1940. Because he was part Jewish on his mother's side, he was in danger of being sent to a concentration camp.

In the fall of 1943, Bohr was smuggled out of the country on a fishing boat in the middle of the night. He made it to England and later the United States, where he worked on the development of the atomic bomb. However, he later joined Einstein in calling for nuclear disarmament.

Edwin Hubble Finds the Universe

THOUGH QUANTUM physics was drawing the attention of many physicists to look inward, toward the atom, others had already turned their attention to the farthest reaches of space in a new and growing scientific field called cosmology. How did the universe begin? Why do stars form? And what is the nature of space and time? Not surprisingly, Einstein's theories played a role in the field's early development.

Albert Einstein had suggested three ways to test his General Theory of Relativity: calculations on the shift of Mercury's orbit (done), measurement of the light from distant stars "bent" by the sun's gravitation (done), and discovery of a "red shift" of light coming from massive stars.

Light has certain wavelike properties. For visible light, red light has a longer wavelength than blue light. Einstein believed that light leaving a massive star would be stretched from a shorter wavelength to a slightly longer wavelength, which he called "red shift." If astronomers could measure the wavelength of light coming from the sun and compare it to the wavelength it should have without gravity, it should confirm his general theory.

In Berlin, Erwin Freundlich, whose own eclipse expedition had been cut short by the war, set out to solve the red shift question. He had earlier suggested that the German scientific establishment honor Einstein's achievement by building a new telescope at the Potsdam Observatory, outside Berlin, to study the question. Construction on the Einstein Tower, designed by architect Erich Mendelsohn, began in 1919 but was not completed until four years later.

Though the Einstein Tower was one of the most advanced observatories of its time, researchers at the Mount Wilson Observatory in California were about to steal the world's attention. A 35-year-old astronomer named Edwin Hubble had "found" the universe. And it was big. Very, very big.

Humans had always known the universe was full of stars. All they had to do was to look up into the night sky. But it wasn't until 1610 that Galileo, using a telescope, figured out that the hazy white ribbon that crossed the heavens, called the Milky Way, was actually billions of additional stars. The Milky Way wasn't something "out there"—we were part of it. Our sun was just one star among all the others. And although many astronomers tried to map the Milky Way, nobody was quite sure what shape it was.

Edwin Hubble had a hunch that our galaxy might not be the only one. In 1924 he trained Mount Wilson's newest telescope—it had a reflecting mirror that was 100 inches across, strong enough to spot the light of a candle from 5,000 miles away—on the blurry Andromeda nebula. (Most astronomers called it M31.) At the time astronomers believed nebulae, which came in all sorts of shapes, were clouds of matter in the process of becoming stars or planets. Hubble discovered that Andromeda was instead another galaxy, and it was 2,500,000 light-years away, so far away that it looked like a tiny, blurry star.

Edwin Hubble (1889–1953)

Edwin Hubble was born in Marshfield, Missouri, in 1889. His father wanted him to be a lawyer, but his passion was astronomy. After college he gave law a try, but later took a job teaching high school physics (and Spanish) in Indiana. Following World War I, he became a staff astronomer at the Mount Wilson Observatory in California.

Hubble was as quirky as he was brilliant. Though he spent only three college years in England, he spoke with a British accent and would often wear a beret and a black cape. Some of the other astronomers thought his behavior was silly, but his work at Mount Wilson brought worldwide attention on the observatory.

The Hubble Space Telescope, carried into orbit aboard the Space Shuttle in 1990, was named in his honor.

Edwin Hubble at his desk, 1940.
Courtesy of the Archives, California Institute of Technology (10.12-20)

After Hubble's announcement in 1924 that the Milky Way wasn't the only galaxy in the universe, astronomers went back and looked at other nebulae and discovered that many were galaxies as well. First they found dozens—then hundreds, and then thousands. (Today astronomers believe there are 100,000,000,000 galaxies in the universe.) By looking at the shapes of all these galaxies, they were also finally able to figure out the shape of the Milky Way. We (on Earth) are on an arm of a giant, swirling galaxy that is 100,000 light-years across.

As remarkable as this discovery was, in 1929 Hubble learned something else. By comparing the red shift of the light coming from various galaxies, he found that the farther away a galaxy was from ours, the faster it moved. (This relationship is called Hubble's Law.) In other words, the universe was expanding like a giant balloon.

The red shifts Hubble measured were not created by the gravitational pull of the galaxies but by their movement. In much the same way gravity could stretch a light beam's wavelength, the wavelength could be stretched longer by having its source move away from an observer very fast, or squished shorter—blue shifted— by moving toward an observer.

Einstein had first opened the door to the idea of an expanding universe in 1917. But he didn't like the idea that the universe (which he thought at the time was only the Milky Way and the empty space beyond it) would expand forever. He thought it was static—stationary, neither expanding nor contracting. After much thought, he added a term to his equations, a "cosmological constant," to make them fit his view of the universe. He later claimed the idea was his greatest mistake. Hubble's 1929 observations appeared to confirm this. Einstein later admitted, "The red shift of distant nebulae has smashed my old construction like a hammer blow."

What Is a Light-Year?

A light-year is not a measure of time, but of distance—the distance traveled by a beam of light in one year. Because light travels at 186,282 miles per second, and there are 31,557,600 seconds in a year (365.25 days), a light-year is 5,878,625,373,184 miles—about 6 *trillion* miles. It takes light from the sun only 8 minutes, 19 seconds to reach Earth. But light from Andromeda takes 2,500,000 years to get here. No wonder it looks so small—it's about 1,500,000,000,000,000,000 miles away!

M31, the galaxy Andromeda.

NASA Chandra Space Telescope Collection

Other Galaxies

ON A clear, dark night you can see the Andromeda galaxy, even without a telescope.

You'll Need
➤ Clear night in November
➤ Constellation map
➤ Binoculars or telescope (optional)

Andromeda is best seen in the month of November, but in the northern hemisphere you can easily see it from October to December. Because Andromeda is faint, you will not be able to see it from a city location—you will need to be in the country, far from any light pollution. Try to go on the night of a new moon, when it is darkest.

To begin, find a star map for the November sky in your area—check online (www.astroviewer. com is good; click "Current Night Sky" and enter your city).

Outside, after dark, locate the constellations Cassiopeia, which is shaped like a big *W*, and Pegasus, which has a large square of stars in the center. Draw (or imagine) a line connecting the left arm of Cassiopeia's *W* to the closest corner of Pegasus's square, as shown.

Andromeda will appear as a dim blur just to the left of the connecting line, midway between these two constellations. You should be able to see both constellations even if the moon is out, but if you have difficulty seeing Andromeda, a pair of binoculars or a telescope may be helpful.

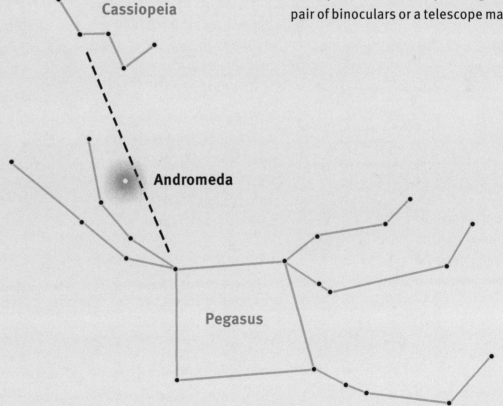

The Expanding Universe

HUBBLE'S LAW says that the farther away a galaxy is from the Milky Way, the faster it moves. To better understand this, you can model the expanding universe in a microwave oven, no telescope required.

You'll Need

➤ Adult supervision
➤ Red and black markers
➤ Peep (or large marshmallow)
➤ Metric ruler
➤ Paper plate
➤ Microwave oven
➤ Calculator

1. Using a red marker, draw a dot on the foot of your Peep.

2. Next, use a black marker and a ruler to draw another dot, 1 centimeter away from the red dot, toward its head.

3. Continue to draw black dots, 1 centimeter apart, up the front of the Peep, until you run out of room.

4. Place the Peep in the center of a paper plate in a microwave oven.

5. Turn the microwave on high for 30 seconds. Watch the Peep through the window. Be ready to pull it out and measure it, but be warned—IT WILL BE VERY HOT!

6. Measure the distance between the red dot and the first black dot. Measure between the red dot and the second black dot, the third dot, the fourth, and so on.

Record your information in the third column of the table below.

7. Calculate the change in distance between the red dot and each black dot. Then calculate the speed at which each black dot moved away from the red dot.

Look at your data and calculations. Imagine that the Milky Way is the red dot and other galaxies are black dots. What can you say about the relationship between how far apart dots/galaxies are and the speed at which they move, relative to each other?

faster it moves away.
Answer: *The farther a galaxy is from the Milky Way, the*

Black Dot Number	Starting Distance to Red Dot	Final Distance to Red Dot (Measured)	Change in Distance from Red Dot (Final – Starting)	Speed of Black Dot (Change ÷ 30 seconds)
1	1 cm	___ cm	___ cm	___ cm / second
2	2 cm	___ cm	___ cm	___ cm / second
3	3 cm	___ cm	___ cm	___ cm / second
4	4 cm	___ cm	___ cm	___ cm / second
5	5 cm	___ cm	___ cm	___ cm / second

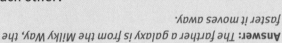

Darkness Descends on Germany

As ALBERT Einstein was shining new light on the nature of the universe, a darkness was descending on Germany. Philipp Lenard's early campaign to discredit relativity was just a small part. The Nazi Party (officially the National Socialist German Workers' Party, which was not socialist) wasn't just interested in silencing Einstein's "Jewish physics"; it wanted to silence him altogether.

On June 24, 1922, Germany's foreign minister, Walther Rathenau, was murdered by two former German army officers as he rode through Berlin in a car. Rathenau had recently signed the Treaty of Rapallo, a peace agreement between Germany and Soviet Russia that the German nationalists despised. What's more, Rathenau was Jewish, and the Nazis blamed the Jews for all of the country's problems.

"A number of people . . . have independently warned me not to stay in Berlin for the time being," Einstein wrote to Planck two weeks later, declining to attend a high-profile scientific conference. But even though he was on the Nazis' hit list, he refused to leave the country. He moved briefly to Kiel, in the far north. Then, five weeks after Rathenau's assassination, Einstein appeared at a pacifist rally in Berlin where speakers denounced the nationalists' violent tactics.

Germany saw a brief letup in the street violence after Adolf Hitler tried, and failed, in November 1923 to overthrow the German leadership in a coup called the Beer Hall Putsch. He was sentenced to five years in prison, though he served less than a year behind bars.

Around this time Einstein was advocating what he called "militant pacifism." Rather than sitting back while nations prepared for war, he said pacifists should actively try to stop war from ever breaking out. In 1925 he signed a document with Mahatma Gandhi, H. G. Wells, and others against compulsory military service—the draft. He later said, "I would absolutely refuse any direct or indirect war service and would try to persuade my friends to do the same, regardless of the reasons for the cause of the war." Some criticized him for not being realistic about Hitler's ultimate plans.

Back in Switzerland, Hans Albert married Frieda Knecht on May 7, 1927. Hans Albert had met Knecht while in college—he graduated in 1926—and had admired her intellect. But their union was not supported by either of his parents. Albert and Mileva thought Knecht was too old (she was nine years older than Hans Albert), unattractive, and unworthy of their son. Sound familiar? Hans Albert was more like his father than Albert admitted. "I tried my best to convince him that marrying her would be crazy," Albert wrote Mileva. "But it seems like he is totally dependent on her, so it was in vain."

The stress of Einstein's life and work finally caught up with him in April 1928, when he collapsed on a visit to Switzerland. Doctors found he had an enlarged heart and ordered bed rest. Elsa knew she would not be able to handle all the work that needed to be done, so she hired a woman named Helen Dukas to be Albert's personal secretary. It was a good match. Dukas

Einstein in Caputh, 1931.
Library of Congress Prints and Photographs Division (LC-USZ-4940)

worked for Einstein the rest of his life—and even longer.

As Einstein's 50th birthday approached in 1929, the city of Berlin suggested buying a summer home for its most famous citizen. But the Nazis, who were gaining positions in government, would have none of it. The Einsteins went ahead and purchased wooded land in nearby Caputh and had a cottage built near the Havel River and Lake Templin. It was a nice retreat from the political ugliness of the capital. His friends bought him a small sailboat as a birthday gift.

"I like living in the new little wooden house enormously, even though I am broke as a result," Einstein wrote to his sister, Maja. "The sailboat, the sweeping view, the solitary fall walks, the relative quiet—it is paradise." He refused to have a telephone installed.

Back in Switzerland, Eduard Einstein entered the University of Zurich, hoping to become a psychiatrist. Before his first year was over, he had a nervous breakdown and was placed in an institution. His father wrote him an encouraging letter. "People are like bicycles. They can keep their balance only as long as they keep moving." But the advice wasn't particularly helpful. Eduard suffered from severe mental illness, most likely schizophrenia, and needed medical help more than advice. He would spend most of the rest of his life in hospitals.

America Calls

THE EINSTEINS were able to briefly escape the tensions at home during a trip to the United States in 1931. After a five-day stop in New York, they sailed south through the Panama Canal on their way to Los Angeles.

Albert Einstein spent the first two months of 1931 as a visiting professor at the California Institute of Technology—Caltech—in Pasadena. While there, the Einsteins took a trip up to Mount Wilson to visit with Edwin Hubble. While being shown around the observatory, Elsa was told that the elaborate equipment was used to determine the shape and nature of the universe. "Oh, my husband does that on the back of an old envelope," she teased.

The couple had even more fun on a visit to Hollywood's Vitagraph Studios. Albert and Elsa were filmed pretending to drive an open car sitting on a soundstage. When the studio later played it back, the Einsteins appeared to be driving around Los Angeles, flying through clouds over the Rocky Mountains, and finally landing in Germany.

Actor Charlie Chaplin later invited them to attend the premiere of his new movie, *City Lights*. When they emerged from the limousine, the crowd went crazy. Nobody could tell who they were more excited to see, Einstein or Chaplin.

In Pasadena, Einstein was visited by physicist Abraham Flexner. He told Einstein of a plan to establish a research institute on the East Coast. Flexner wanted Einstein to join the faculty. The institute would not be like a college, but rather a "think tank" where the world's great scientists would have the time and resources to work on their theories. Einstein had been down this road before with the Kaiser Wilhelm Institute, and at first he passed, saying he was like a tree that was too old to be transplanted. But he didn't rule out the idea entirely.

From California the Einsteins headed east, stopping at tourist destinations along the way. In Arizona they saw the Grand Canyon and visited with the Hopi Indians. They admired Albert's pacifism and gave him the honorary name of the "Great Relative." Elsa used the trip to raise money for several children's charities—she charged $1 for her husband's autograph and $5 for a photo with him, which she kept track of in a small booklet.

Their visit to America was not all vacation. In New York, Einstein gave a lecture to the New History Society where he proposed a new idea called the "2% Manifesto." In it he encouraged 2 percent of those who had been drafted to refuse military service as conscientious objectors. (A conscientious objector is somebody who refuses military service for moral or religious reasons.) Einstein felt that by filling

Einstein at the Mount Wilson observatory.
Courtesy of the Archives, California Institute of Technology (1.6-5)

Final Days in Germany

At the Grand Canyon (from left to right): Walther Mayer, Helen Dukas, Elsa Einstein, unknown woman, Albert Einstein, unknown man, 1931.
Courtesy of the Leo Baeck Institute, New York (F 5316L)

jails and providing a public face to pacifism, the strategy could prevent future wars. The 2% Manifesto was based on Henry David Thoreau's *Civil Disobedience* and the work of Mahatma Gandhi, whom Einstein admired. But developments in Germany had many wondering if it was practical, or wise.

THE EINSTEINS returned to Germany in the spring. But Hitler was gaining more supporters month by month, and it became increasingly clear that they could not stay in Berlin forever.

The Einsteins returned to California in the winter of 1931–1932, for Einstein to lecture at Caltech. While there, Einstein accepted Flexner's offer to spend six months of every year in Princeton at the newly created Institute for Advanced Study. Flexner asked Einstein to name his salary, and Einstein suggested $3,000 a year. That was far below what Flexner had expected, so he offered him $15,000. Einstein was set to return in the fall.

But not everyone wanted Einstein living in America. A conservative group called the Woman Patriot Corporation asked the US State Department to investigate whether, as a pacifist, he was part of an "anarcho-communist" group intent on destroying the military. They even claimed he was more dangerous than Joseph Stalin, the leader of Soviet Russia.

At first Einstein thought it was funny, and he sent a letter to the group. "Never yet have I experienced from the fair sex such energetic rejection of all advances," he wrote, "or if I have, never so many at once." But several days later he was asked to come by the US embassy in Berlin. There he was questioned about his motives for going to the United States. "Your countrymen invited me," he shot back. "Yes, begged me. If I am to enter your country as a suspect, I don't want to go at all. If you don't want to give me a visa, please say so." He then walked out without an answer. The embassy backed down and gave him a visa the next day.

Einstein knew what the future held. The world was moving toward war. Later, when leaving their Caputh home in December 1932, Albert locked the door and turned to Elsa. "Take a very good look at it. You will never see it again." They took 30 bags of luggage with them.

On January 30, 1933, after the Einsteins had arrived in Pasadena, the world learned that Hitler had become German chancellor. Returning to Germany was now unthinkable. "As long as I have any choice, I will only stay in a country where political liberty, toleration, and equality of all citizens before the law are the rule," Einstein announced on March 11. "These conditions do not [exist] in Germany at the present time."

The German Gestapo, Hitler's secret police, broke into the villa in Caputh, claiming they were looking for hidden weapons. They

The Big Bang

When Edwin Hubble determined that the universe was expanding, a big question arose: expanding from what? Could everything in the universe be tracked back to one giant explosion of mass and energy? Russian mathematician Alexander Friedmann had already suggested that idea in 1922. Belgian astronomer (and Catholic priest) Georges Lemaître came up with a similar theory in 1927. He believed that the universe might have started as a "primeval atom," a single *something* that violently expanded billions of years ago, like a giant firework.

When he first heard about Lemaître's theory, Einstein couldn't accept it. But, after hearing Lemaître talk in 1933, Einstein jumped up and gave him a round of applause. "This is the most beautiful and satisfactory explanation of creation to which I have ever listened."

The term "Big Bang" was first used by English astronomer Fred Hoyle in 1950. Though the Big Bang Theory is widely accepted today, the physics behind the current theory is very different from the theory Lemaître originally proposed.

found only a bread knife. Albert's sailboat was seized and later sold. The Nazis froze the couple's bank account, and in early summer the Gestapo kicked in the door of the Einsteins' Berlin apartment. While their daughter Margot, Helen Dukas, and a housekeeper looked on, the thugs carted off everything.

Well, almost everything. All of Einstein's papers had vanished.

Albert Einstein becomes a US citizen, October 1, 1940, with Judge Phillip Forman. Library of Congress Prints and Photographs Division (LC-DIG-ppmsca-05649)

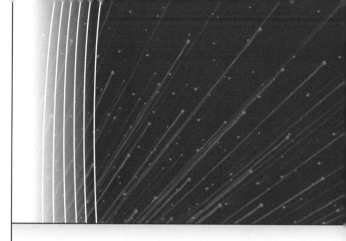

America and the Bomb

1933–1945

RUDOLF KAYSER, ILSE Einstein's new husband, had connections in Germany's anti-Nazi underground. He had heard rumors that the Nazis planned to raid his father-in-law's home and apartment. As a writer and editor, he knew Einstein's personal papers were valuable, and perhaps even dangerous, to the regime. At the very least, Hitler might get some satisfaction by destroying them.

Kayser was determined not to let the papers fall into the wrong hands. He met with officials at the French embassy in Berlin, and, before the Nazis arrived, had Einstein's notebooks and manuscripts packed into trunks and smuggled into the embassy. From there they were eventually taken by diplomatic pouch, safe from German hands, to Paris. There, they waited.

> "In America, the development of the individual and his creative powers is possible, and that, to me, is the most valuable asset in life."
>
> —Einstein in "I Am an American," 1940

Queen Elisabeth of Belgium.
Courtesy of the Leo Baeck Institute, New York (F 5338)

Le Coq-sur-Mer

THE EINSTEINS could not go home to Germany, but they did return to Europe. Though Einstein had kept his Swiss citizenship when he moved to Berlin in 1914, he was made a German citizen, too, when he was elected to the Prussian Academy. After the war the government had made it official by giving him a passport. When Albert and Elsa arrived in Antwerp, Belgium, on March 29, 1933, they immediately drove to Brussels, where Albert marched into the German consulate, surrendered his passport, and renounced his citizenship.

Einstein had learned the Prussian Academy planned to expel him along with other Jewish scientists, so he resigned his seat in the academy as well.

In Berlin, Max Planck tried to defend his friend. "Even though in political matters a deep gulf divides us," he wrote, "I am absolutely certain that in the centuries to come Einstein will be celebrated as one of the brightest stars that ever shined on our academy."

While figuring out what to do next, the Einsteins rented a cottage in Le Coq-sur-Mer on the Belgian coast. During earlier trips to Brussels to attend the Solvay conferences, Albert had become friends with Belgium's King Albert and Queen Elisabeth. He and the queen had played the violin together, and she enjoyed his company so much they wrote to each other often.

The king had two armed bodyguards watch the Einsteins' new home. Back in Germany a photo of Albert had appeared in a Nazi "enemies of the state" booklet with a caption that read, "Not yet hanged." They had also placed a 20,000-mark bounty (about $5,000—or $90,000 today) on his head. Soon others joined the Einsteins—Helen Dukas and Walther Mayer arrived in April. Margot and her husband fled to Paris, though Ilse and her husband stayed in Berlin.

For Jews in Germany, life grew worse by the day. On April 7, Jews were officially barred from holding any government jobs. Fourteen Jewish Nobel laureates fled the country. Einstein famously predicted, "If and when war comes, Hitler will realize the harm he has done by driving out Jewish scientists." On April 25, the Nazis enacted the Law Against the Overcrowding of German Schools and Institutions of Higher Learning, limiting all but a few Jews from attending any schools or colleges. And on May 10, the first book burning was held in Berlin. Forty thousand people watched as piles of books by Jewish authors, including Einstein's *Relativity*, went up in flames in front of the State Opera House.

Einstein wrote to Max Born, "I have now been promoted to an 'evil monster' in Germany, and all my money has been taken away from me. But I console myself with the thought that the latter would soon be gone anyway."

By this time it was clear that Hitler had military plans beyond Germany's borders. Einstein was asked whether he still supported pacifism, and he surprised many by changing his position. "Were I a Belgian, I would not, in the present circumstances, refuse military service. Rather, I would enter such service cheerfully in the belief that I should thereby be helping to save European civilization," he wrote. Several pacifist groups became angry with him.

From the United States, the Institute for Advanced Study offered to make Einstein's position full time and permanent. After much consideration—he'd received offers from other universities—he accepted.

In May, Einstein went to Zurich to see Mileva and Eduard. Albert stayed with Mileva, then visited his son at the mental institution where he had been hospitalized. He brought his violin, hoping to play a duet with Eduard as they once had. Eduard was too distracted or nervous to play the piano. It was the last time Albert would ever see Eduard or Mileva.

Albert and Elsa left Belgium and stayed for some months in Oxford, England, in the home of a member of Parliament. While there Einstein met with Winston Churchill, who for years had been warning the world of Hitler's sinister intentions.

Finally, on October 7, 1933, Albert and Elsa sailed out of Southampton aboard the *Westmoreland*, bound for New York. Helen Dukas and Walther Mayer went with them. They never returned to Europe.

Princeton

THERE WAS a welcoming parade organized for the Einsteins when they arrived in New York on October 17, but they hardly felt like celebrating. Instead, Abraham Flexner took the couple off the oceanliner by tugboat, snuck them past the crowds, and drove them directly to Princeton. Flexner then announced, "All Dr. Einstein wants is to be left in peace and quiet."

That statement was more Flexner's wish than Einstein's command. Flexner wanted Einstein to avoid controversy, or even attention. But Einstein's move was a big deal. The French physicist Paul Langevin explained it best: "It is as important an event as would be the transfer of the Vatican from Rome to the New World. The pope of physics has moved, and the United States will now become the center of the natural sciences."

After a brief stay at a local hotel, the Einsteins moved into a rented home on Library

Place. The institute set up a temporary office in Princeton's mathematics building. When asked what supplies he needed, Einstein replied, "A desk or table, a chair, paper and pencils. Oh yes, and a large wastebasket, so I can throw away all my mistakes."

Though some in Princeton were concerned (or excited) about having an international celebrity in town, the Einsteins settled into a quiet, small-town life. At Christmastime a group from the First Presbyterian Church stopped by their home while caroling, and Albert rushed out with his violin to join them. (He had done the same on Halloween when several children showed up to play a trick; they were so surprised they forgot why they had come.)

Einstein obviously enjoyed the newfound freedom that life in the United States provided. He wrote to Queen Elisabeth how much he appreciated "the democratic trait among the [American] people. No one humbles himself before another person or class." Even with the president.

The Einsteins were invited to spend the night at the White House on January 24–25, 1934. The invitation was arranged by Rabbi Stephen Wise so that Einstein could speak to Franklin Roosevelt, who had been in office less than a year, about the plight of European Jews. The president and Einstein enjoyed talking about their love of sailing and discussed developments in Germany. Roosevelt suggested to Einstein that he should be awarded US citizenship by an act of Congress, but Einstein insisted that his and Elsa's applications be treated the same way any other refugees' would.

Several months later Elsa learned that her daughter Ilse was gravely ill with leukemia in Paris. Ilse had recently fled Berlin and moved in with her sister, Margot. Elsa sailed for Europe and was able to see Ilse before she died in July. (Ilse's husband, Rudolph Kayser, returned to the Netherlands after her death.)

On her trip back to the United States, Elsa brought her husband's papers, which Margot

A Famous Pen Pal

Children from all over the world loved to write letters to Einstein, and he would often write back. In 1951 a six-year-old girl named Ann wrote, "I saw your picture in the paper. I think you ought to have a haircut, so you can look better." A young admirer from South Africa asked him for an autographed picture in 1946, and after Einstein sent it she wrote back to confess that she was a girl—she hadn't stated this in her first letter. "I hate dresses and dances and all the kind of rot girls usually like. I much prefer horses and riding. Long ago, before I wanted to become a scientist, I wanted to be a jockey and ride horses in races. But that was ages ago, now," she said. "I hope you will not think any less of me for being a girl!" Einstein wrote back, "I do not mind that you are a girl, but the main thing is that you yourself do not mind. There is no reason for it." Another girl, Barbara, wrote to him in 1943 to tell him about her troubles with math. "Do not worry about your difficulties with mathematics," he responded. "I can assure you mine are still greater."

and Rudolph had retrieved from the embassy and stored in their Paris apartment. Two Princeton neighbors, Andrew and Carolyn Blackwood, were traveling on the same ship and helped Elsa get the papers through customs—Elsa had worried they might be confiscated because she was not a US citizen, so the Blackwoods claimed they were theirs, "material acquired in Europe for scholarly purposes."

Elsa returned to America a changed woman. Those who knew her say she aged a great deal that spring. Her daughter Margot joined the Einsteins in Princeton in the summer of 1934, after separating from her husband.

The Einsteins bought a home at 112 Mercer Street in August 1935. They had a large picture window installed in Albert's office upstairs so he could look out over the backyard garden and think. Margot and Helen Dukas lived there as well, along with a dog named Chico, a cat named Tiger, and (eventually) a parrot named Bibo. The small yellow house was several blocks from the institute, and Albert enjoyed the walk back and forth from his office every day. Sometimes, deep in thought, he would get lost, but there was always a helpful student or citizen to point him in the right direction.

A few of the children in the neighborhood were particularly happy to have a genius nearby. Eight-year-old Adelaide Delong showed up at the Einsteins' home one day with a plate of fudge, then asked Albert if he could help her with her math homework. She returned many times before her parents found out and apologized to Einstein. "That's quite unnecessary. I'm learning just as much from your child as she is learning from me," he told them, then

The Einsteins' Princeton home, 112 Mercer Street.
Courtesy Historical Society of Princeton (A_9_g_002)

added, smiling, "Do you know she tried to bribe me with candy?"

Einstein seemed to bond with the children of Princeton. He would often amuse them by showing that he could wiggle his ears. And they never seemed to want too much from him, like so many adults did, other than to talk. Why didn't he wear socks, many wondered. "I've reached an age when, if somebody tells me to wear socks, I don't have to," he told them.

But Albert's new, happy life in Princeton didn't last long. In the fall of 1935 Elsa learned that she was very sick. Both her heart and her kidneys were failing. Her health gradually declined over the next year, and she died at home on December 20, 1936.

War on the Horizon

MEANWHILE IN Germany, Hitler and his followers expanded their persecution of anyone they felt was an enemy of the state. In the fall of 1935, the Nuremberg Laws made all German Jews non-citizens and forbade them from marrying non-Jews. On March 12, 1938, Germany annexed Austria, making it part of the Third Reich. (Hitler had been born in the German-speaking country.)

And then on the night of November 9, 1938, following the murder of a German diplomat in Paris, Nazi mobs attacked Jews throughout Germany and Austria. Over 1,600 synagogues were looted or burned, and thousands of Jewish-owned businesses were destroyed. Many people were beaten to death, and far more were arrested and sent to concentration camps. The tragic event became known as *Kristallnacht*—the Night of Broken Glass—because of all the shattered store windows.

Einstein's sister, Maja, who was living in Florence, Italy, emigrated to America in 1939. Italy, under the control of Benito Mussolini and the National Fascist Party, was following Hitler's lead and it wouldn't have been safe for her to stay. Maja's husband, Paul Winteler, was denied entry to the United States, so he moved to Geneva, Switzerland.

Maja moved into the home on Mercer Street. For the first time since Elsa had died, Einstein felt truly happy. Nobody understood him quite like his sister. And by this time, they even had the same hair.

Several months before his sister arrived, Albert's son Hans and his family also immigrated to the United States. Hans Albert and Frieda now had two young sons, Bernhard and Klaus. (Klaus died of diphtheria a few months after they arrived.) Hans Albert had a job studying soil conservation in South Carolina. Considering the stormy relationship he

Burning synagogue in Baden-Baden during Kristallnacht. Courtesy of the Leo Baeck Institute, New York (F 229)

had with his father, it was a safe distance from Princeton. They could easily visit but keep their distance, too.

Einstein returned to his Unified Field Theory with new vigor. "I'm still working passionately," he wrote to his old Zurich friend, Heinrich Zangger, "though most of my intellectual off-spring are ending up prematurely in the cemetery of disappointed hopes." But Einstein felt this was his mission, one that young and unknown physicists wouldn't have the freedom to pursue. Einstein had the good will and reputation to spend years looking for something he might never find.

In addition to his scientific work, Einstein spent a considerable amount of time helping Jews who were fleeing Europe. In the late 1930s he received thousands of letters from refugees, asking for help. He did what he could. He wrote letters of support for immigration applications, filled out forms for the US State Department, and looked for American sponsors for families hoping to come to the United States. "The pressure on us from the poor people over there is such that one almost despairs," he wrote to Michele Besso.

And as bad as the news was, it was about to get much worse. In December 1938, German scientists in Berlin achieved something that even Einstein had long thought impossible: they had split an atom.

Two Letters

NIELS BOHR was still living in Denmark when he learned through a chain of colleagues that Otto Hahn and Fritz Strassmann, working at the Kaiser Wilhelm Institute, had split uranium atoms. They had done this by firing neutrons at the atoms. In the process a large amount of energy had been released, confirming Einstein's energy-to-mass conversion formula, $E = mc^2$. Physicist Lise Meitner, who had fled to Sweden from Germany, gave the process the name that is used to this day: she called it fission.

Bohr came to Princeton in January 1939 to inform Einstein and others. If there was any good news, it was that the Germans had not yet figured out how to harness this new energy source. It was just an experiment in a laboratory. But some physicists believed that it could one day lead to a new type of weapon.

Leó Szilárd, a friend of Einstein's from Berlin, was worried most of all. In 1933, while walking through London and thinking, he came up with the concept of a nuclear chain reaction that would unleash a tremendous amount of energy. He had done some research on his own, hoping to learn more. But when

Leó Szilárd. Argonne National Laboratory, courtesy AIP Emilio Segre Visual Archives, gift of William Numeroff

he learned about the Germans' success with uranium, he knew he had to act.

On July 15, 1939, Szilárd and physicist Eugene Wigner drove out to Long Island, New York, to find Einstein. They found their old friend in a cabin in Peconic where he was vacationing. There, on the screened porch, they explained how a chain reaction could be started.

"I never thought of that," Einstein replied. But once he *had* thought about it with Szilárd and Wigner, he understood the problem. Anyone with access to uranium could build a powerful bomb. Where could Germany find this uranium? The Congo, in central Africa, which was then a Belgian colony. Szilárd had led Einstein to the conclusion he wanted: he needed to contact Queen Elisabeth to stop Germany from getting to the Congo's uranium. (King Albert had died in 1934 in a mountain-climbing accident.)

The three men did not want to act without the support of the American president. Luckily, Albert knew him, too. On August 2, Einstein signed a letter that was to be hand-delivered to Franklin Roosevelt by Alexander Sachs, one of the president's economic advisers. It said, in part:

Some recent work ... leads me to expect that the element uranium may be turned into a new and important source of energy in the

immediate future. ... This new phenomenon would also lead to ... extremely powerful bombs of a new type. ... A single bomb of this type, carried by boat and exploded in a port, might very well destroy the whole port together with some of the surrounding territory. ... You may think it desirable to have some permanent contact maintained between the administration and the group of physicists working on chain reactions in America.

Sachs did not deliver the letter until October 11, six weeks after Germany invaded Poland. After he read it, Roosevelt immediately formed the Advisory Committee on Uranium. A month later the committee reported its findings to the president, though no immediate action was taken. On March 7, 1940, Einstein wrote another letter. This one was addressed to Sachs, claiming, "Since the outbreak of the war, interest in uranium has intensified in Germany," then warned that the United States should again look at the issues involved.

Sachs delivered the second letter to Roosevelt a week later. The Advisory Committee on Uranium was expanded, but not much was accomplished for another year and a half. Roosevelt finally launched the Manhattan Project, the US effort to create a nuclear bomb, on December 6, 1941. The next morning, Japanese planes bombed Pearl Harbor.

The War and the Bomb

As AMAZING and ridiculous as it sounds, Albert Einstein, the man who prodded the president into developing the nuclear bomb, was not allowed to be part of the Manhattan Project. The director of the FBI, J. Edgar Hoover, had labeled Einstein a security risk because of his involvement with socialist and peace groups. "In view of this radical background, this office would not recommend the employment of Dr. Einstein on matters of a secret nature," he wrote.

So, while most of his colleagues in America were going to work in mysterious locations—Oak Ridge, Tennessee, and Los Alamos, New Mexico—Einstein stayed in Princeton. On June 22, 1940, he took the citizenship test to become an American citizen. He passed. Margot and Helen Dukas did the same. And on October 1, all three were sworn in as new US citizens along with 86 other immigrants at a courthouse in Trenton, New Jersey. (Albert did, however, maintain his Swiss citizenship.) A month later they all voted in their first American election.

After the United States entered World War II in late 1941, Einstein did his part to support the effort. He assisted the US Navy in its development of explosives to destroy torpedoes. He sometimes joked that he was "the only one in

Einstein speaks to an American audience, 1940.
Library of Congress Prints and Photographs Division (LC-H22-D-9005)

Enrico Fermi with the atomic pile at the University of Chicago, 1942.

Courtesy AIP Emilio Segre Visual Archives

the navy who didn't have to cut his hair." And in 1944 he donated a recent paper on "bivector fields" as well as a handwritten copy of his 1905 paper on relativity to be auctioned off for a war bond drive. The papers earned $11.5 million for the cause, including $6.5 million for the rela-tivity paper. (Both were later donated to the Library of Congress.)

Leó Szilárd had gone off to Chicago, where he helped Italian physicist Enrico Fermi create the first nuclear chain reaction. They built a pile of alternating uranium and graphite bricks in a racketball court at the University of Chicago. The pile had a hole running through the center. According to their calculations, in the final step they would slide a control rod into this hole, creating what was known as "critical mass."

This is how all nuclear chain reactions work—radioactive material is brought together in a tight bundle, and neutrons released from the center control rods split the atoms around them, which then release more neutrons that split more atoms, and so on, and so on. If it happens slowly, heat is released, but if it happens quickly, so much energy is released it explodes.

On December 2, 1942, less than a year after Pearl Harbor, Fermi and others gathered in the court under the stands of the football stadium. They watched as control rods were slowly inserted into the pile. Sensors picked up an increase in neutrons, more and more the farther the rod was pushed. The chain reaction had begun. Twenty-eight minutes after they started, the control rods were removed and the chain reaction stopped.

Though Einstein didn't work on the Man-hattan Project, he was smart enough to figure out what was going on from the few things he did know. He started to worry about what he had helped set in motion. He wrote to Niels Bohr: "The politicians do not appreciate the possibilities and consequently do not know the extent of the menace." Bohr had just recently been smuggled out of Denmark, which was under German control, and was on his way to the United States with a fake passport. If anyone asked, he was Nicholas Baker. On his way to Los Alamos, New Mexico, Bohr stopped in Princeton. He told Einstein a few details about what was going on . . . and told him to keep quiet.

In Los Alamos the Manhattan Project, under the direction of Robert Oppenheimer (a former Einstein colleague at the Institute for Advanced Study), was using Fermi's discovery to build a powerful new bomb. In 1944 they began preparing a test site in the southern desert of New Mexico. By the spring of 1945 it was ready.

That March, Leó Szilárd also had second thoughts about the project. He visited Einstein and urged him to write another letter to President Roosevelt.

I understand that [Szilárd] now is greatly concerned about the lack of adequate contact between scientists that are now doing this work and those members of your cabinet who are responsible for formulating

Chain Reaction

A CHAIN REACTION occurs when too much radioactive material, a critical mass, is brought too close to other radioactive material. In this activity, you will model what happens by using dominoes, where each domino represents a uranium atom.

You'll Need
➤ Set of dominoes   ➤ Level table

Start by arranging a group of dominoes in a pattern where each one is placed farther apart than the length of a domino.

Now knock over a single domino. What happens?

Not much. But now place additional dominoes—uranium atoms—*between* all of the dominoes you arranged earlier. The dominoes should now be very close.

Knock over a single domino again, and watch what happens this time.

In the experiment performed by Enrico Fermi, the piles of uranium and graphite were like the first set of dominoes you set up. When he inserted the control rods into the pile, it was like adding the additional dominoes.

Winston Churchill, Franklin Roosevelt, and Joseph Stalin at the Yalta Conference, February 1945, just two months before Roosevelt's death.

Library of Congress Prints and Photographs Division (LC-DIG-ppmsca-05649)

policy. . . . I wish to express the hope that you will be able to give his presentation of the case your personal attention.

The war was almost over in Europe—Germany would surrender on May 7—so Szilárd knew the bomb would not be needed there. He wanted to ask the president not to drop the bomb on Japan on moral grounds—he suspected that it would be used on a civilian target. But the meeting never happened. Einstein's letter was delivered to the White House, but Roosevelt didn't read it before he died on April 12. It was later found, unopened, in his office.

On July 16, 1945, a giant fireball rose into the early morning sky over the New Mexico desert. Oppenheimer had successfully detonated the world's first atomic bomb. It had the explosive power of 20,000 tons of TNT.

Three weeks later, on August 6, a US plane dropped an atomic bomb on Hiroshima, Japan. When the news came over the radio, Einstein was taking a nap. Helen Dukas told him after he woke up. He recoiled, saying in German, "*Oh, Weh.*" (Oh, woe.)

On August 9, a second bomb was dropped on Nagasaki. Six days later, Japan surrendered. World War II was over.

Mushroom cloud over Nagasaki, Japan, August 9, 1945.

Library of Congress Prints and Photographs Division (LC-USZ62-36452)

8

Standing Up for Peace and Human Rights

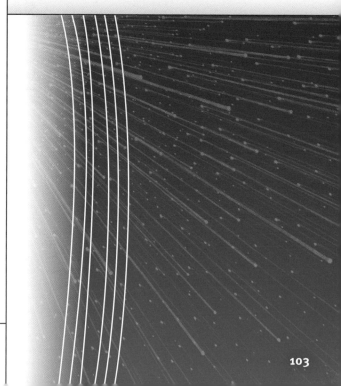

1945–1955

> *"I have become a kind of enfant terrible [pest] in my new homeland because of my inability to keep silent and swallow everything that happens here."*
>
> —Einstein to Queen Elisabeth of Belgium, 1954

ALBERT EINSTEIN WAS horrified. The war was barely over and he, based on his 1939 letter and his famous equation, was being given primary credit for the development of the atomic bomb. He wrote a letter to his son, "Dear [Hans] Albert! My scientific work has no more than a very indirect connection to the atomic bomb."

More than 80,000 people had perished in Hiroshima, and 70,000 in Nagasaki. Tens of thousands more would die in the years to come from the aftereffects of radiation. And people were hailing this as a *triumph* of science?

Einstein at Princeton, 1947. "The most heartrending change was in his eyes.... The livid face was clearly being consumed from the inside out." —Anatonia Vallentin

Library of Congress Prints and Photographs Division (LC-USZ62-60242)

After the War

EINSTEIN OFFICIALLY retired from the Institute for Advanced Study in 1945, though he continued to keep an office at the institute where he would work on his Unified Field Theory. He could still be seen walking around Princeton, sometimes stopping in the middle of an intersection to debate a point with a colleague while cars passed around him.

Back in Zurich, things were not going well for Mileva or Eduard. In 1939, Mileva had to sell the two investment homes, and in 1946 Albert bought her third home, the one she lived in, to keep her from losing it to a stranger. In May that year she slipped on some ice while headed for the Burghölzli mental hospital to visit Eduard. She lay unconscious in the snow, where she was later found near death.

Though she recovered from the fall, Mileva had a stroke on May 24, 1948. She was paralyzed and confined to a bed, where she died on August 4. People later found 85,000 Swiss francs in her mattress. The money was turned over to the hospital for Eduard's care.

Maja also had a stroke in 1948. Bedridden, she stayed at the home on Mercer Street for the next three years. Albert read to his sister every evening until she died on June 25, 1951. Einstein was heartbroken. "I miss her more than can be imagined," he wrote.

Einstein spent more and more time on his 17-foot sailboat, named the *Tinef*, which is Yiddish for "junk" or "worthless." He would sail around alone on Princeton's Lake Carnegie. He never wore a lifejacket, though he had never learned to swim.

As much as Einstein may have wanted to retire from public life, he felt a responsibility to speak out about issues that affected the nation and the world. On July 1, 1946, *Time* magazine put Einstein on its cover, with a mushroom cloud in the background along with his famous equation. If he was going to be the face of the Bomb, he felt responsible to stop it.

Ban the Bomb

AFTER THE war was over, Robert Oppenheimer returned to New Jersey to direct the Institute for Advanced Study. When he first met Einstein in 1935, he wrote to his brother, proclaiming, "Einstein is completely cuckoo." Now the famed scientist was publicly regretting ever getting involved in the Manhattan Project, which Oppenheimer had directed.

Einstein was named the first chairman of the Emergency Committee of Atomic Scientists in May 1946. (Leó Szilárd was also a founding member.) The committee believed in arms control enforced by a "supranational" world government, one that was stronger than the newly formed United Nations. "The unleashed power of the atom bomb has changed everything except our modes of thinking, and thus we drift toward unparalleled catastrophes," Einstein warned in one of the ECAS's first fund-raising telegrams.

Many, like Oppenheimer, tried to dismiss Einstein as old and out of touch. A dreamer, not a realist. But Einstein would not shut up. Had he ever? In March 1947 he told *Newsweek* magazine, "Had I known that the Germans would not succeed in producing an atomic bomb, I never would have lifted a finger." And he challenged his colleagues as well. In 1948 he told the *New York Times*:

> *We scientists, whose tragic destiny has been to help make the methods of annihilation even more gruesome and more effective, must consider it our solemn and transcendent duty to do all in our power to prevent these weapons from being used for the brutal purposes for which they were intended.*

What about the Soviet Union? people wondered. Though it had been an ally of the United States during the war, now it was challenging western democracies across Europe. What if it got the bomb?

Sailboat Challenge

EINSTEIN LOVED to sail—he called it "the sport that demands the least energy." When he bought a boat in Princeton, he named it the *Tinef*—Yiddish for "worthless" or "junk"—as a joke.

This activity will test your boatbuilding skills. Your material? Worthless junk!

You'll Need

➤ 1 sheet thin cardboard, 8 inches square
➤ 1 sheet aluminum foil, 8 inches square
➤ 2 drinking straws
➤ Tape
➤ Scissors
➤ 100 pennies (2 rolls)
➤ Large bowl of water

Your challenge is to build a boat that will float in a bowl of water, using only the items listed. The tape can be used to patch holes or hold pieces of foil, cardboard, and straws together, but you cannot use it to create new parts.

Once you have built your boat, float it in the middle of a large bowl of water. Then, one by one, add pennies to the boat until it sinks. How many coins could it hold?

Can you think of a way to improve your design? Build it!

Sailing in Lake Zurich.

Einsteinium

In 1952 the United States detonated a new type of bomb, a hydrogen bomb that used fusion, over the Bikini Islands in the South Pacific. After the blast, researchers found a new radioactive element on coral samples pulled from the rubble. It had an atomic number of 99 and was the heaviest element ever found to date. Shortly after Einstein died in 1955, it was given the name einsteinium in his honor. One wonders what the scientist would have thought—he opposed the hydrogen bomb that created it.

That question was answered on August 29, 1949. The Soviet Union detonated its first atomic bomb in Kazakhstan. Einstein's idealistic suggestions were pushed aside as the cold war—the 40 years of tension between western democracies and the Communist bloc of Eastern Europe—took off.

Some began to say that Einstein wasn't just naive, he was dangerous. In 1950 Mississippi congressman John Rankin was the first to denounce Einstein on the floor of the US House of Representatives. "Ever since he published his book on relativity to try to convince the world that light had weight," he ranted, "he has capitalized on his reputation as a scientist . . . and has been engaged in communistic activities."

Civil Rights

CONGRESSMAN RANKIN'S reference to "communistic activities" was not just about nuclear weapons policy, but something even closer to home: civil rights. As much as Albert Einstein loved America, he was deeply troubled by the discrimination faced by African Americans in the United States.

Back in 1937, Marian Anderson, a famous opera contralto, had come to Princeton for a concert at the McCarter Theater. Because she was black, Anderson was refused a room at the local Nassau Inn. When Einstein learned of this, he invited her to stay at his home on Mercer Street, and she accepted. The two bonded over their mutual love of music, and they became good friends. Every time she visited Princeton, up until his death, she would stay at his home. But his kindness shocked many who demanded segregation in the United States.

Princeton, like most US cities and towns, was segregated by race. (At the time, African American students were barred from attending Princeton University.) It had a large black population, but they were mostly confined to one neighborhood, known as Witherspoon for the main street that ran through it. When Einstein walked to a local hospital he had to pass through Witherspoon, where he would chat with people out on their front steps and porches. Here he learned about the racial injustices suffered by those in this community.

In January 1946, Einstein authored an essay titled "The Negro Question" for *Pageant* magazine. "[Americans'] sense of equality and human dignity is mainly limited to men of white skin," he wrote. "The more I feel like an American, the more this situation pains me." The only solution, he felt, was for people like him to speak out.

That May he was invited to Lincoln University, an all-black college west of Philadelphia, Pennsylvania. Einstein gave a lecture to students on relativity, received an honorary degree, and spoke to the graduates. "I do not believe there is a way in which this deeply entrenched evil [racism] can be quickly healed," he said. "But until this goal is reached, there is no greater satisfaction for a just and well-meaning person than the knowledge that he has devoted his best energies to the services of the good cause."

Israel

ANOTHER CAUSE close to Albert Einstein's heart in the final years of his life was the establishment of a Jewish homeland. His first trip to the United States, in 1921, was to raise money for the World Zionist Organization. Now, following World War II, the cause seemed even more important.

While everyone knew Hitler's followers were intent on persecuting and killing Jews, many did not know how far they had gone until after the war was over. Six million Jews had been murdered throughout Europe, as had gypsies, Slavs, homosexuals, Jehovah's Witnesses, the disabled, and anyone else who didn't figure into the German notion of Aryan purity. Many of Einstein's extended family were among the Third Reich's victims.

A Historic Concert

Two years after she first met Einstein, Marian Anderson was denied the chance to perform an Easter Sunday concert at Constitution Hall in Washington, DC. The conservative Daughters of the American Revolution, who owned the hall, would not let an African American perform in its segregated theater.

Angry, First Lady Eleanor Roosevelt resigned from the DAR and persuaded the Secretary of the Interior to let Anderson perform on the steps of the Lincoln Memorial. More than 75,000 people came to hear her open with a familiar song, "America."

My country, 'tis of thee,
Sweet land of liberty, of thee I sing.
Land where my fathers died,
Land of the pilgrims' pride,
From every mountainside, let freedom ring!

Interior Secretary Harold Ickes congratulates Marian Anderson at the Lincoln Memorial concert, April 1939.
Library of Congress Prints and Photographs Division (LC-H22-D-6300)

Zionists believed that the best way to prevent such a tragedy in the future was to establish a homeland in the Middle East. Many had fled to Palestine before the war, and it was here that they wanted to establish the state of Israel.

Einstein supported a safe haven for Jewish refugees, though he did not believe it should be at the expense of Palestinians who already lived in the region. But when Israel was established on May 14, 1948, Einstein gave in. "I have never considered the idea of a state a good one," he wrote. "But now there is no going back, and one has to fight it out."

Chaim Weizmann, the man who had organized Einstein's first US tour, became Israel's first president in 1949. Unlike in the United States, the presidency in Israel is largely a ceremonial post. Instead, the prime minister runs the government. That post was held by David Ben-Gurion.

After Weizmann died on November 9, 1952, Ben-Gurion was pressured to offer the presidency to Einstein. Ben-Gurion was nervous. "Tell me what to do if he says yes," he asked his adviser, Yitzhak Navon. "I have to offer the post to him because it is impossible not to. But if he accepts, we are in for trouble."

But Einstein wasn't interested. At first he was amused, laughing about it with Margot and Helen Dukas. Once he figured out the proper way to decline the offer, which was to wait until after Ben-Gurion officially asked, he told Margot, "If I were to be president, sometimes I would have to say to the Israeli people things they would not like to hear." Einstein had never been good at *not* speaking his mind.

Albert Einstein and David Ben-Gurion, May 1951.

Alan Windsor Richards, Princeton, courtesy of the Leo Baeck Institute, New York (F 5343A)

McCarthyism

As THE Cold War heated up, so did fear in the United States. The Soviet Union now had the bomb. Representatives and senators were demanding to know who might be a communist spy. Einstein, with his passionate advocacy for a world government and nuclear disarmament, was an easy target—or so they thought.

The "Red Scare"—the witch hunt for suspected communists in government, entertainment, and education—grew first out of the House Un-American Activities Committee (HUAC). The congressional committee had been around since the late 1930s, but not until the late 1940s did it become a powerful, destructive force. Starting in 1947, it began calling Hollywood actors, writers, and producers to testify about communists in the entertainment industry. People were blacklisted—put on "do not hire" lists—for refusing to testify. Hundreds of careers and lives were destroyed.

But it didn't stop there. In 1948 HUAC began looking for Soviet spies in government. Congressman Richard Nixon, who would one day become president, gained national attention for attacking Alger Hiss, who worked in the US State Department.

To Einstein the Red Scare looked all too familiar. The same way Jews, pacifists, and socialists had been blamed for Germany's defeat in World War I, now liberals, intellectuals, and socialists were being targeted as threats to the American way of life.

The US Congress and Senate have the power to force anyone to appear before them to answer questions, the same way a court of law does. But Americans also have the right to refuse to testify against themselves, guaranteed by the Fifth Amendment of the US Constitution. They also have the right to think and say whatever they believe without being punished by the government.

Albert Einstein was a firm believer in intellectual and personal freedom. And he wasn't afraid to say so publicly. "Every intellectual who is called before one of the committees ought to refuse to testify . . . in the interest of the cultural welfare of his country," he wrote in an open letter to schoolteacher William Frauenglass in 1953. (Frauenglass had been called before the US Senate to testify about communist influence in high schools.) "Refusal to testify must be based on the assertion that it is shameful for a blameless citizen to submit to such an inquisition and that this kind of inquisition violates the spirit of the Constitution."

Wisconsin senator Joseph McCarthy was outraged. He had been holding his own hearings in the US Senate. "Anyone who advises Americans to keep secret information which they may have about spies and saboteurs is himself an enemy of America," he bellowed. McCarthy's willingness to destroy anyone he disagreed with by abusing his power as a senator gave the Red Scare its more common name: McCarthyism.

Einstein wouldn't be bullied. He was a popular figure in America, and he knew his opinion mattered. Three years earlier, when African American intellectual W. E. B. DuBois was on trial on charges of acting as an illegal foreign agent for his involvement with the Peace Information Center, Einstein offered to appear with him as a character witness. The government then backed down.

Then in 1953 the Red Scare came to Princeton. The Atomic Energy Commission revoked Robert Oppenheimer's security clearance, claiming that the man who had developed the weapon that ended World War II could not be trusted with nuclear secrets. But that wasn't enough for his critics—they wanted him removed from the Institute for Advanced Study as well. Einstein spoke in defense of Oppenheimer. He convinced every member of the institute to sign a petition in Oppenheimer's defense. Oppenheimer kept his job. (He later called Einstein "the nicest man I've ever known.")

In 1954 Einstein summed up his thoughts about the frightened mob mentality that led to injustices like the Red Scare: "In order to be a perfect member of a flock of sheep, one has to be, foremost, a sheep."

Final Days

ALBERT EINSTEIN was nearing the end of his long and eventful life. "I am like a run-down old car—something is wrong in every corner,"

Wisconsin senator Joseph McCarthy, April 1951.
Wisconsin Historical Society (8006)

Toying with the Principle of Equivalence

A‌LL HIS life, Albert Einstein enjoyed logic puzzles and toys. In his final days, he amused himself and his guests with a simple toy that demonstrated the Principle of Equivalence. He had received it as a gift for his 70th birthday. You can build an inexpensive version of this toy to see if you can solve the riddle.

You'll Need
➤ Long, thin rubber band
➤ Scissors
➤ Tape
➤ Billiard ball (or heavy ball about the same size)
➤ Empty toilet paper tube

Start by cutting a thin rubber band into one long piece. Tape one end of the rubber band to a billiard ball. Be sure to use plenty of tape so that it stays attached.

Feed the other end of the rubber band through an empty toilet paper tube. Tape the loose end of the band to the outside of the cardboard tube. Do not stretch it, but do not let it hang loose inside the tube, either.

Now lift the toy by its tube. The ball should hang down from the rubber band, not sit on top.

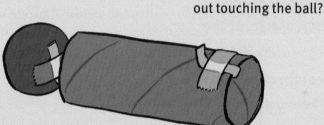

Here's the puzzle: Knowing what you know about the Principle of Equivalence, how can you get the ball to return to the end of the tube without touching the ball?

Answer: Hold the toy high in the air over a carpeted floor. Let go of the toy. Like the man falling off the building, neither the ball nor the tube "feel" their own weight as they fall, so there is no force stretching out the rubber band. This allows the band to pull the ball and the tube back together.

he said. "But life is still worthwhile as long as I can still work."

Hans Albert and his family had moved to California in 1947, where he taught civil engineering at Berkeley. But still, he felt closer to his father than he had in a long time. They sent each other friendly letters. "It is a joy for me to have a son who has inherited the main traits of my personality," Einstein wrote.

In the spring of 1955 Einstein's old friend, Michele Besso, died in Geneva. "He has departed from this strange world a little ahead of me," Einstein wrote to Besso's family. "That means nothing—for us believing physicists, the distinction between past, present, and future is only a stubborn illusion, although a convincing one."

On April 13, 1955, Einstein collapsed in the bathroom of his Mercer Street home. A heart problem that he had suffered with for years had finally caught up to him. At first he refused to go to the hospital. "I want to go when I want," he told Helen Dukas. "It is tasteless to prolong life artificially. I have done my share; it is time to go. I will do it elegantly." But over the next few days the pain got worse. Margot called Hans Albert, who flew to Princeton. On April 15, the 76-year-old Einstein was taken to Princeton Hospital.

On the morning of April 17, Albert felt better and asked Dukas to bring him his glasses and a pen and paper. With Hans Albert, Margot, and Dukas by his bedside, he tried to give the Unified Field Theory a few last shots. "If only I had more mathematics," he told them.

At 1:15 AM the next day, Einstein awoke, muttered a few words in German, then died. His abdominal aorta had ruptured. It was almost 50 years to the day since he had completed his paper on the Special Theory of Relativity.

Condolences, public and private, arrived from neighbors and from around the globe. Mathematician and philosopher Bertrand Russell said of his friend, "Einstein was not only a great scientist, he was a great man. He stood for peace in a world drifting toward war. He remained sane in a mad world, and liberal in a world of fanatics."

According to his wishes, Einstein was cremated and his ashes were scattered at a spot he had chosen on the Delaware River. Only his family knew where. His violin was given to his grandson Bernhard.

Afterword

Einstein Lives On

In his will, Albert Einstein stated that he did not want his home to become a museum or shrine. To this day the house at 112 Mercer Street is a private home. Not everything, however, went according to his final wishes.

Einstein's Brain

Though his family did not know it at the time, when Einstein's body was given an autopsy, the doctor who performed it removed his brain. Thomas Harvey said he wanted to study it to understand the source of Einstein's genius.

Harvey had not gotten the family's permission to do this. And they might never have known except that Harvey's son mentioned it at school a few days later. His teacher had asked her fifth-graders about recent news, and when one girl brought up Einstein's death, the young Harvey blurted out, "My dad's got his brain."

The Einsteins complained, but Harvey convinced them that it was all in the service of science. Yet Harvey had no background in brain research. Over the years he sent off slides of tissue to any scientist who could persuade him, but nothing much was learned. Harvey eventually moved to Kansas where he kept the remaining pieces in two glass cookie jars on his office shelf.

Not until the late 1990s was any serious research done on Einstein's brain. Scientists discovered slight differences in his brain structure: he had a parietal lobe—responsible for mathematical and spatial reasoning—that was 15 percent larger than normal. However, it was not enough to definitively prove where his genius originated.

Einstein's Family

ACCORDING TO Einstein's will, both Helen Dukas and his friend Otto Nathan became trustees of the scientist's letters and papers. For years, Dukas carefully organized his papers and guarded his reputation. Though she helped write several books about her former boss, she prevented everyone who saw his files from revealing that Albert and Mileva had had a daughter before they were married. In December 1981, just months before Dukas died, Einstein's papers were transferred to Hebrew University, where they are held today.

Hans Albert Einstein taught hydraulic engineering at the University of California at Berkeley for the rest of his life. Frida, his wife, passed away in October 1958. Hans Albert remarried a year later, to Elizabeth Roboz. On July 26, 1973, Hans Albert died of a heart attack while attending a conference in Woods Hole, Massachusetts. His son Bernhard, who had become a physicist like his grandfather, died in

2008. Evelyn, Hans Albert and Frida's adopted daughter, passed away in April 2011.

Eduard Einstein remained in the Burghölzli psychiatric clinic until he had a stroke in 1964. He died in Zurich the following year on October 25, 1965.

Margot Einstein lived at the home on Mercer Street until she passed away in July 1986.

Einstein's Scientific Legacy

ALBERT EINSTEIN'S revolutionary theories have held up well in the decades since his death. Black holes and the Big Bang—mere theories when Einstein was alive—are today foundations of modern cosmology.

NASA has studied relativity at length. In 1976, it launched Gravity Probe A in an effort to confirm the Principle of Equivalence. The probe carried an extremely sensitive clock that could be compared to another back on Earth. By analyzing its data, scientists confirmed Einstein's theory of how space-time changes in a gravitational field.

In 2004, NASA launched Gravity Probe B to further measure the warping of space-time around the Earth. It orbited the planet for a year and a half, taking detailed measurements using highly accurate gyroscopes. Again, the data confirmed Einstein's General Theory of Relativity.

Another confirmation of Einstein's theories can be found in your own pocket. If you have a phone that uses the global positioning system (GPS), it has been programmed to account for the warping of space-time. After all, it receives signals from satellites high above the Earth, and their internal clocks run at a different rate than the clock in your phone. It might seem like too small a difference to worry about, but, given the speed of light, a small change in time can mean a large difference in the distance light travels during that time. Without a correction for relativity, your GPS could be several miles off *every day*.

Will all of Einstein's theories hold up to future study? If history can tell us one thing, you don't have to be a genius to bet on Einstein getting it right.

Resources

For information on all quotations found in this book, visit www.chicagoreviewpress.com/educationalresources.

Books for Further Study

Calaprice, Alice. *The Einstein Almanac*. Baltimore, MD: Johns Hopkins University Press, 2005.

Calaprice, Alice (ed.). *The Ultimate Quotable Einstein*. Princeton, NJ: Princeton University Press, 2011.

Delano, Marfé Ferguson. *Genius: A Photobiography of Albert Einstein*. Washington, DC: National Geographic Society, 2008.

Einstein, Albert. *Relativity: The Special and General Theory*. New York: Plume, 2006.

Gardner, Martin. *Relativity Simply Explained*. Mineola, NY: Dover, 1997.

Isaacson, Walter. *Einstein: The Life of a Genius*. New York: Collins Design, 2009.

Wishinsky, Frieda. *Albert Einstein*. New York: DK Publishing, 2005.

Yeats, Tabatha. *Albert Einstein: The Miracle Mind*. New York: Sterling, 2007.

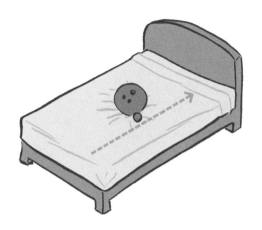

Websites and Places to Visit

SEVERAL OF these websites are located in German-speaking countries, so you may have to find the "English" button on the page to be able to read them.

EINSTEIN MUSEUM

Helvetiaplatz 5
CH-3005 Bern
Switzerland
www.bhm.ch/en/exhibitions/einstein
-museum

This is the only museum in the world dedicated to both Einstein's life and his scientific legacy. Visitors will find artifacts from the Einstein family and the Swiss Patent Office.

EINSTEIN HOUSE, BERN

Kramgasse 49
Postfach 638
3000 Bern
Switzerland
www.einstein-bern.ch

Albert and Mileva Einstein lived in this Bern apartment from 1903 to 1905. Hans Albert was born here and Albert wrote his "Miracle Year" papers in the front parlor. Managed by the Albert Einstein Society, it has been restored to its 1905 appearance.

EINSTEIN SUMMER HOUSE, CAPUTH

Am Waldram 15–17
14548 Caputh
Germany
www.einsteinsommerhaus.de

Einstein was forced to abandon this home outside Berlin when Hitler came to power in Germany. Today it is open to select visitors by appointment.

ALBERT EINSTEIN MEMORIAL STATUE

National Academy of Sciences Building
2101 Constitution Avenue, NW
Washington, DC 20418
www.nasonline.org/about-nas/visiting-nas/
nas-building/the-einstein-memorial.html

This oversized statue of Einstein was sculpted by Robert Berks and unveiled in 1979. It is located just north of the Vietnam Veterans Memorial on the grounds of the National Academy of Sciences.

MOUNT WILSON OBSERVATORY

466 Foothill Blvd, #327
La Canada, CA 91011
www.mtwilson.edu

Edwin Hubble used this observatory, located in the mountains above Pasadena, California, to study the universe. Albert Einstein visited whenever he came to California. Tours are available from April through November.

BRADBURY SCIENCE MUSEUM

Los Alamos National Laboratory
Mail Stop C330
Los Alamos, NM 87545
www.lanl.gov/museum/index.shtml

Einstein was not directly involved with the Manhattan Project, but most of his professional colleagues in America were. This museum, located on the laboratory campus where the atomic bomb was developed, explores their work.

ALBERT EINSTEIN ARCHIVES

Hebrew University of Jerusalem
www.albert-einstein.org

All of Albert Einstein's personal papers are located at the Albert Einstein Archives in Jeru-salem. Though not open to the general public, visitors are welcome to browse his papers at the archive's website.

INSTITUTE FOR ADVANCED STUDY

Executive Drive
Princeton, NJ 08540
www.ias.edu/people/einstein

Albert Einstein worked at the Institute for Advanced Study for the last twenty years of his life. It is not open for visits, but its website tells the history of Einstein's role at the institute in its early years.

AIP CENTER FOR HISTORY AND PHYSICS

www.aip.org/history/einstein

The American Institute for Physics has a website dedicated to Albert Einstein's memory. See family photos, read letters from Einstein and others, and find links to other Einstein resources.

AMERICAN MUSEUM OF NATURAL HISTORY

www.amnh.org/exhibitions/einstein

The museum's Einstein exhibit closed in 2003, but the online portion is still online, and very interesting.

Index

Italicized page numbers indicate illustrations.

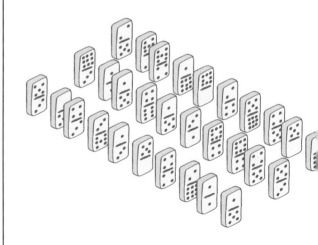

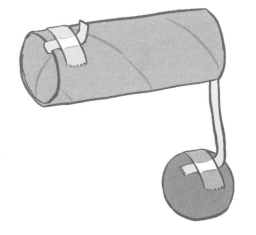

Isaac Newton and Physics for Kids

His Life and Ideas with 21 Activities

Kerrie Logan Hollihan

978-1-55652-778-4
$16.95 (CAN $18.95)
Also available in e-book formats

"Hollihan introduces readers to the scientific brilliance, as well as the social isolation, of this giant figure, blending a readable narrative with an attractive format that incorporates maps, diagrams, historical photographs, and physics activities."

—*Booklist*

"Written for children, this book is also a great resource for teachers and parents."

—*Connect*

"Sanitized, sculpted, and politically correct stories of human luminaries are typically fed to schoolchildren. Author Kerrie Logan Hollihan, however, offers middle-grade readers a refreshing and comprehensive look at the man touted as the greatest scientist who ever lived."

—*BookLoons*

Thomas Edison for Kids

His Life and Ideas, 21 Activities

Laurie Carlson

978-1-55652-584-1
$16.95 (CAN $18.95)
Also available in e-book formats

"A lively biography of one of the most creative and inventive minds in history."

—*Booklist*

"A solid addition to the Edison shelf."

—*Kirkus Reviews*

"Approachable and educational . . . a valuable resource for units on electricity, communication, or inventors."

—*VOYA*

"An engaging introduction to the life and work of inventor Thomas Edison."

—*KLIATT*

"Blends the historical and the practical beautifully."

—*Library Media Connection*

"This book will inspire kids to be inventors and scientists."

—*Parents Express*

"This cool book will inspire the curious minds of a new generation."

—*Charlotte Parent*

CHICAGO REVIEW PRESS

Distributed by IPG
www.ipgbook.com

www.chicagoreviewpress.com

Available at your favorite bookstore, by calling (800) 888-4741, or at www.chicagoreviewpress.com

Exploring the Solar System

A History with 22 Activities

Revised Edition

Mary Kay Carson

978-1-55652-715-9
$17.95 (CAN $22.95)
Also available in e-book formats

"Outstanding.... Will sweep readers up in the wonder and excitement."
—*Kirkus Reviews*

"A real science book that should interest children in the solar system."
—*St. Louis Post-Dispatch*

"Well-written history of space exploration."
—*Seattle Times*

"Inventive, fun, and thought-provoking."
—*Austin American-Statesman*

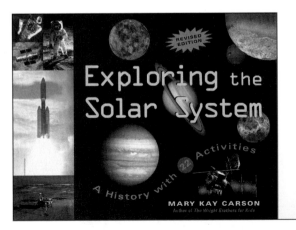

Galileo for Kids

His Life and Ideas, 25 Activities

Richard Panchyk
Foreword by Buzz Aldrin

978-1-55652-566-7
$18.95 (CAN $20.95)
Also available in e-book formats

"Fascinating... full of useful and insightful information. A good read."
—*Science Books & Films*

"A must-have."
—*KLIATT*

"A good choice for those interested in integrating history and science curriculums."
—*School Library Journal*

"Delightful and engaging as readers learn to appreciate Galileo's genius and integrity."
—*NSTA Recommends*

CHICAGO REVIEW PRESS

Distributed by IPG
www.ipgbook.com

www.chicagoreviewpress.com

Available at your favorite bookstore, by calling (800) 888-4741, or at www.chicagoreviewpress.com